From the Farm to Fast Food:
My Adventures during the Great Depression and Beyond

Raymond C. Schmidt

Copyright © 2012 Raymond C. Schmidt

All rights reserved. Except for classroom educational purposes, no part of the publication may be reproduced or distributed in any form or by any means or stored in a database or retrieval system without the prior consent of the author.

Requests for permission should be sent to:
Amy Ray
Email: amy@maray.org

For educational purposes, the author grants teachers and their students the right to duplicate this book for their individual use and that of their students. Only one copy, digital or print, can be made per student and teacher.

ISBN: 1478364513
ISBN-13: 978-1478364511

About the Author

Ray Schmidt was born the eldest son of German-speaking farmers in 1922 in western North Dakota. While growing up, he and his family experienced the hardships of the Great Depression firsthand. Like most young people, Ray embarked on various professions initially, including the music business. An accomplished self-taught accordionist who plays by ear, he and one of his bands, the Blue Flames, cut a polka record in the early 1940s.

Eventually Ray got into the farming business himself in North Dakota. Then, in 1964, he and his wife, Marie, decided to take a chance on the next big thing: fast food. Their venture led them to Miles City, Montana, a dusty cattle town, where they purchased a small Dairy Queen. With the help of Marie and their eight children, the Schmidts were able to make the business a huge success. It became one of the largest and top-performing Dairy Queens in Montana. He and his son, Ray Schmidt, Jr., later went on to launch and operate a number of restaurants in Montana and Utah. Today, Ray and Marie live in Richland, Washington, near three of their daughters whom Ray regales with funny stories and harasses endlessly with political debates.

FOREWORD

This is a collection, or recollection, if you will, of events, incidents, adventures, and misadventures in and around my early life. It is in response to many requests by my curious children, children-in-law, and grandchildren who appear to be fascinated or puzzled by remarks of mine related to my childhood. They are in need of explanation as some border on the bizarre as they relate to today's world and society. Lifestyles were different then, and in some respects better than today (in my opinion anyway, which isn't shared by many, if anyone at all). So I'll ramble down memory lane.

    I am not a professional writer, so these stories follow no specific sequence. They are just random and maybe sort of mixed up. Not all stories that come to mind will entertain and amuse or astound some. However, I do think many of them are highly educational—especially for today's generation. Have you ever had to plant explosives to mine your own coal to heat your house? Climb up some posts to keep your neighborhood's phone lines up and running? How about dig your own well or cut ice out of a river to cool your food? Kill, skin, dry, and can animals to feed your family? You never know. In a post-apocalyptic world, you might want to know how that's done. Other stories about driving underage, smoking on a lunch break, and joining a band will sound more familiar but still different. And, of course, there is a love story. I hope you enjoy your reading and learn something in the process.

Turning Blue But Pulling Through

Much of this book explains what I experienced during the Great Depression. Poverty in America. This is horrible. I saw it at its worst during the Great Depression. I was a teenager then and did not know what to make of all this. It didn't look or feel right. Relief, welfare, seed loans, feed loans, farm foreclosures, and auction sales with hardly anyone bidding. People crying, losing their homes and with nowhere to go. Drought, dust, tumbleweeds, sand dunes, starving livestock, billions of grasshoppers munching on the siding of houses and tool handles after having destroyed the grain fields. Stores and banks closed and shuttered.

The nationwide unemployment number was nearing 25 percent. In other words, one of every four workers was jobless. Groups of men hung around businesses in hopes of getting a day's work unloading a railroad car of lumber or whatever. I watched as hobos by the hundreds rode on top of boxcars on the trains. Families, some with infants, rode inside. The doors were open. The sanitation in the cars was likely a problem. Some people were going east, and others going west in search of jobs or to live with relatives somewhere for some means of survival. You could see from the looks of the women's faces that they had been crying. Trainmen apparently gave up kicking them off, so they let them ride.

It wasn't always this way. The 1920s were better than the 1930s. I was born in 1922. The place: The home of my mother's parents, in North Dakota in a small town called Dickinson. I was the second of 11 children born to Barbara and George Schmidt. Supposedly, it was a traumatic event. I didn't come easy and almost didn't make it. I "turned blue," whatever that means. A doctor was summoned to assist the midwife who delivered me, and for sure some serious prayers were whispered by my grandma, rosary in hand, as well as holy water sprinkled on the entire scene. (Grandma did things like that. So did a lot of Catholics I have known throughout my life.) But I "pulled through," as the saying goes.

Here's Barbara Armbrust, later to be my mom. Who would have thought this sassy beauty would one day slap around 11 bratty kids (me and my 10 brothers and sisters)?

I do not know for sure, but it's likely George must have hauled pregnant Barbara and their two-year-old daughter Marian in a horse drawn wagon from the farm he leased 40 miles northwest of Dickinson for my birthing, as there were no automobiles then. This would have been too hard a trip for one day, so there must have been an overnight stop at a midway point, likely at his dad, Carl Schmidt's farm, north of Dickinson.

Grandpa Carl had a spacious two-story home with a porch with pillars (see the following photo). It was an impressive structure out on the prairie in those days. There was also a summer kitchen of matching architectural style adjacent to the house. Summer kitchens were used for cooking, laundry, and ironing during hot summer months to keep heat out of the house. It was especially useful for as Grandpa Carl and his wife, my Grandma Eva, had eight sons and only one daughter, my godmother, Mary Eva. Grandpa Carl was active in political circles and a county commissioner, a position he held until his sudden death in his 60s. I remember him paying my Dad's taxes to keep us from losing our farm during the Great Depression. Carl was a thinker, pacing the floor back and forth, hands clasped behind his back, usually deep in thought.

A good looking bunch: The Carl Schmidt family, except for Ludwig, who was the oldest and died in the flu epidemic of 1918. Standing on the porch of their fine new home on the prairie are Grandma and Grandpa Schmidt (to the right) and their only daughter, Mary Eva (my godmother). Seated are my many uncles and my father, who is the second from the left in the back the row.

My Dreams as a Young Boy: From Ponies to Planes

Sometime between my somewhat tumultuous birth and my 4th birthday, my family moved to a farm known as the Bullinger place, which was named after the original homesteader. The Bullinger house was made of stone. It consisted of two bedrooms, a living room, and kitchen-dining room with a cellar accessible by a trap door. There was a steep ladder-like set of stairs that led into the cellar. The shelving in the cellar provided space for canned veggies and beef. The dirt floor was ideal for keeping spuds, carrots, beets, turnips, and other root vegetables. These were for sustaining life on the prairie during snowbound winters when roads were blocked for months, which was an often occurrence. The cellar was also seen as a torture chamber for Marian, my oldest sister, and me. Our mother threatened to and sometimes did incarcerate us there for fighting and for disobedience. (Sad to say, but my wife and I would later subject our kids to this same form of child abuse in a similar facility in one of our houses. We did not have the option of locking them in their rooms without their iPads.)

Other buildings included a stone henhouse (also known as a chicken coop) a garage-workshop with a sod roof, and a wood frame barn with stalls for Prince and Charlie, our ever-faithful but at times ornery, team of black gelding plow horses with white starred foreheads. There was also a space for several milk cows and calves. Several cats lived in there also, and a hayloft above was a great place for kids to play.

Several farm magazines came by mail to our house: *The Dakota Farmer, Farm Journal,* and *Successful Farming* among others. In one of them, an ad with a picture of a spotted pony got my attention. "Win This Pony," the ad read. "Send your name and address in with this coupon and you may be the lucky winner!" I had Mother read the ad to me. Then I looked for and found an envelope, cut out the coupon, and asked her to send it in for me. She did.

I then started planning for the pony's arrival. I would stable him on the east side of the garage where it was sunny in the morning and had shade in the afternoon and was not windy. I began hauling hay with my little red wagon from the haystack by the barn to the new pony's home. I loaded the hay, tying it down with twine, pulling it up an incline to the garage, back and forth for days. I also provided buckets for oats and water. The new pony would be very happy.

One day my hay hauling was delayed by the excitement of seeing airplanes for the first time in my life. They were coming right for this hay-hauling kid! Looking northeast, not one, but two, open cockpit biplanes came roaring over, low and slow. I saw the "aviators" in their leather caps and goggles as they went by, heading southwest. I yelled for Mother to come quick, and we watched them until they were specks in the sky.

Suddenly, I lost interest in the pony. I decided I would be an aviator; no doubt about it. This would be the most exciting life ever, flying through the sky at great speed over the countryside. People would look up at that daredevil Raymond Schmidt and wave at me as I zoomed by. I would be a "big shot," yes sir! To heck with the dumb pony. Let some other kid win it.

The flying thing persisted in my mind as I grew older. How do these things fly, I wondered? They have wings, but they don't flap like the birds. One day when I went with Dad to town, I stopped at the library and checked out the book *The Theory of Flight* and studied it. I learned about lift, air flow over and under the wings, and so on. Soon I was sure I could fly a plane the first time at the controls. Thereafter, I completed a Civil Air Patrol test. (The Civil Air Patrol was a sort of Homeland Security-type of initiative going on at the time.) But I never heard back, so I must have flunked.

The flying bug in me got squished one Sunday afternoon years later, though. I went to the local airport and gave Carl Sorenson, a flight instructor, $5 for a 30-minute ride in a two-seater Piper Cub plane. One minute after the wheels lifted off the runway and 100 feet up, I knew that I did not like flying. It was not as I had envisioned it at all. Instead of the sensation of forward speed, we just seemed to hang up there in one spot, and the countryside passed slowly below. Not what I had in mind. Carl did a few aerobatic dips and turns, which my belly didn't like. Adding to the scenario was a light thundershower with wind, necessitating a full power landing in the grass instead of the runway because of the crosswind. Goodbye, flying Ace Raymond Schmidt. It was time to pursue a new dream. I did fly later in life in my 60s. Grant Johnson, a restaurant contractor I was working with, turned the controls of his twin-engine Beech Baron over to me at one point in our flight. "Keep it level, straight and at 13,000 feet," he instructed. "I've got some numbers I need to work on." Grant then busied himself with a calculator and glanced at the dial occasionally.

"Want me to land this for you, Grant?" I asked him as our destination came into view.

"No, maybe next time, Ray," he replied. I never won the pony either.

School Rules:
Don't Mess with Your Teacher

In 1927, my sister Marian and I started school. The school was a forlorn-looking wooden structure in need of paint and other maintenance. It featured a potbellied coal stove and surrounding metal jacket to protect us kids from getting burned and the Fayette school district from getting sued, I guess, although suing was not in vogue in those days. Lawyers were cheap by today's standards but still not affordable.

The path to this institution of learning led toward my Uncle Anton Jaeger's house, where we were joined by our cousins Rose, Kate, Megan, Eva, and Tony. From there it was a one mile, pleasant scenic country walk in fair weather or a Prince-and-Charlie-powered wagon or sled in bad weather. We liked these Jaeger cousins, Rose, Kate, and Megan because they were older and took care of us. They had been attending classes and were aware of the school's hazards and adversities—something which Marian and I were about to learn.

The school's teacher was Miss Mabel Delkrin, a middle-aged, tough, husky gal, up to the task before her. This was a challenging gig for her, but she seemed to actually enjoy it. The students were mostly Russian. The Skachenkos, Spelevoys, Osacheskys, and Valenchenkos are some of the names of families that come to mind in addition to Jaegers and Schmidts. The kids were a diverse bunch, mostly older and in their early teens.

Many of them should have been out of there at the ages they were. However, attending school in the community was not a serious matter, but a place to send the kids when they were not needed to clean the barn or butcher a pig or haul stones to build a chicken coop. Hauling kids to school was a nuisance. But the law said you have to send the kids to school, so okay. They would be at their desks now and then.

Recess was terror time for me and my cousins. We were first graders. John, George, and Joe, who were from a Russian family and were brothers, were older, big, burly guys who carried jack knives. They would chase us three wimps down the ravine into the brush, catch us, pin us to the ground, pull down our pants, and threaten to castrate us, releasing us only when we begged for mercy and promised not to tell "bitch Delkrin" or our parents or we would really lose our little twins. They would also stuff snow into our pants, leaving us looking like we peed in them as it melted.

Big bad John did meet his match one day, so to speak. He and some of the other guys made "match shooters," which consisted of an empty thread spool with a rubber band around it. After inserting a farmer's match (a match with a wood stem) they were able to aim, fire, and ignite whatever they shot at. The matches would hit the chalkboard with a whack, ignite, and fall aflame to the floor.

These sneaky attacks always occurred when the room was quiet, and most, but apparently not all, students were busily studying or writing. Suddenly "wham!" and a little fire was burning on the floor by Miss Delkrin's desk, startling everyone in the room, including the kid who had pulled off this stunt. He acted most surprised of all, like, "Who would do such a thing?"

But, the wily, feisty Miss Delkrin had a good idea who. She had grown tired of extinguishing numerous farmer-stick blazes, although they weren't too serious a threat to the safety of her pupils or the school district's old building. She became annoyed by this nonsensical disruption of her classroom and felt it was her duty as a paid employee to not put up with it any longer. So she watched, but pretended not to be watching, and one quiet afternoon, sure enough, she saw out of the corner of her eye the sneaky John loading his spool with a farmer match, pulling back on the rubber band like a bowman taking aim at a ten-point buck (or however many points bucks have). As she suspected, the culprit was big bad burley John. . . Perfect! The match hit its target and ignited, and Miss Delkrin was on her way to John's desk. Let the kids put out the damn fire. She was on a mission. "Hand it over," she demanded, extending her palm, hoping John wouldn't hand over the spool. And he didn't. "Go to hell," he sneered back at her.

What happened after that was kind of a blur, a wrasslin' match like no other: A burly Russian, 16-year-old third grader and a tough female teacher establishing her dominance in this country school classroom. She had him on the floor and in no time at all, started back to her desk, farmer match shooter in hand. "You goddamn Rooshin," the defeated and humiliated John whispered after her. But his whisper was too loud, which was a bad mistake, because Miss Delkrin heard it.

She returned and grabbing a handful of John's thick black hair, she proceeded to slap the crap out of him with the other hand. He tried to escape this onslaught to no avail as she grabbed another handful of curls and kept whacking. This woman was not an ordinary goddamn Rooshin. "Get the broom and dust pan and clean up the floor [his hair]," she growled at her subdued pupil. And he did. John never came back to school after this incident. By now I wasn't so sure I wanted to be educated either. Are this and the recess-thing how going to school would be for eight years?

When My Family Moved

A view of my father's farm in recent years: It is now called the Schmidt Ranch and owned and operated by one of my brother's children. The tallest landmark visible from the farm was Teepee Butte. It can be seen in the background.

The traumatic first year of my schooling was behind me, and what an experience it was. As I reflected back on it, I thought perhaps the Russian concept of not going to school seemed appealing. To hell with it. Who needs to put up with this just to learn to read and write? I had my own issue with Miss Delkrin, that being the appropriate form of the number 4, which is not resolved to this day. She said it was sort of a chair upside down. Well, why upside down? What's the sense in that? When my arithmetic papers crossed her desk, the 4s were right side up! Legs down, back rest up! So be it! (An early sign of bullheadedness and more to come.)

My legs-up-4s hang-up went with me to my new school. I had no better results with my next teacher, Ellen Scharr. We had moved, but not far, one mile south. Dad George purchased the 480 acres adjacent to the Bullinger 160 acres. Now we were up to 640 a section. Lots of work for a dad with a son whom he will enslave for the next 15 years, was my thinking. Those vast fields to the south and west in need of plowing, harrowing, seeding, harvesting, bindering, shocking, threshing, with teams of horses pulling machinery, Raymond sitting on that hard metal seat, bouncing up and down, yelling "Giddyup, giddyup, Lady, you lazy ol' nag, giddyup," from sunup till sunset, every day of the week, except Sunday.

Sunday was another form of agony: Going to confession and communion and fasting from midnight until we got back home from the 10 A.M. Mass. Sunday afternoon the horses needed to be "grained," or fed oats, so as to give them more energy for the week ahead. I could see it all; 640 acres of work.

Moving meant that I could longer look to the northeast every day and see the Fayette Mercantile where sweet candy mints were behind glass in a little wooden keg, taunting me, and bottles of Nehi Orange Crush and strawberry and grape and lemon pop stood in icy water inside the red Coca-Cola cooler. I went to that store often with mother and Marian with the baskets of eggs gathered from the coop, stolen from the chickens. The eggs were to be traded for staples, such a sugar, salt, flour, jar lids, and things we didn't grow in the garden. Mrs. Little, who owned and ran the store, always slipped a bag of goodies into mom's order for us kids. Mrs. Little was a sweet adorable lady. She was "the high-class stylish lady from back east" revered by everyone in the community. She always had several pencils stuck in her hair like big city storekeepers. More about Mrs. Little later.

How to Build Your Own House, Family Style

A house is under construction on a little knoll at the new farmstead. Uncles Florian, Carl, and Pete Schmidt are on hand with handsaws and hammers, eagerly going at it. Building structures is in their blood. The amateur homebuilding uncles are doing great but are in a hurry. Haying time is coming soon and will take priority over building their brother George's house. House building is more fun than sitting on a hard hot steel mower seat, constantly keeping an eye on the sickle so it doesn't run into stones or bird nests or gophers and watching the hay fall into a "gathering buncher." Then you had to pull a lever thousands of times on the buncher, dumping the hay into rows for easier raking into piles after a few days of drying while hoping it didn't rain and screw everything up. Two of the uncles are measuring and sawing components, two other uncles are nailing them up, and I am the gopher running in between, catching hell for not keeping up with hustling boards to them. What did they expect from a six year old? A Charles Atlas? (For those of you who do not know who

Charles Atlas is, think Arnold Schwarzenegger.) I loved the smell of new wood, especially cedar shingles. It made me consider abandoning being an aviator and becoming a carpenter instead, and later in my life I did became sort of a woodworker.

The "house" was not actually built to be a house at all. It was temporary living quarters until money flowed in from the abundant crops this additional acreage would generate, at which time a finer and larger home would be constructed on a knoll nearby. The house would be sort of like Grandpa Carl's, with the pillars and dormers and shutters, and so on, at which time this building would become grain storage space, filled with grain from the bountiful harvests to come. It was a grandiose dream, I must say. You can't fault anyone for dreaming. But Mother Nature and other economic factors intervened, so it was never to be. It functioned as a house for decades, and stands today in disrepair. Whenever I see it, it conjures up memories good and bad.

Moving into the new house presented some inconveniences. The chickens, cows, pigs, and the pregnant, soon-to-give-birth cat, remained a mile north at the Bullinger place. Their new home had not yet been built. Our horses, Prince and Charlie, likewise were without quarters. Their barn hadn't been moved either, but they were fully engaged in the moving process, trotting back and forth, pulling the wagonloads of furniture, most of which was in need of repair and/or refinishing, almost not worthy of a space in a new house. But since it was to become a granary, what the heck? Might as well use the furniture up, then throw it away and replace it with mahogany and fine oak when the real Grandpa-style house was built.

The need-right-away things made up another wagonload: canned goods and last year's potatoes from that damn cellar. "Good riddance," I said to myself as the last sack of spuds was hoisted up the cellar stairs. I remembered the namesday parties where Catholics celebrated to honor the saints after which they were named and the revelers danced atop that cellar. I felt like dancing on it now. I hated that dungeon. Goodbye cellar. You ain't never gonna see me down there no more in your blackness, you beast!

Still Moving:
Our First Tractor and Mousie the Cat

A delivery truck turned into the driveway of the new Schmidt farmstead one day. The driver unloaded a large powerful-looking McCormick-Deering Model 15 30 tractor. It looked used, and it was, but wasn't very old and looked to be okay. The numbers meant horsepower: 15 HP (horse power) pulling power and 30 HP belt power for threshing. Engineers figured all these horse-power numbers out, I suppose.

Now we had a tractor. Our horses Prince and Charlie should be happy. Mr. Malmstad, the owner of the company that owned the tractor, brought it for Dad to try out. "Work it for a week or two. If you think you can use it and like it, I'll make you a heck of a good deal," he said. Malmstad was a "wheeler dealer." He knew Dad would have to get more power to handle the additional acreage. Now instead of three separate horse-drawn operations, tilling, seeding and harrowing, it could be done in one operation. Imagine that.

But the first task of this 15 30 was to move the barn from the Bullinger place to the new location. Dad and his brother-in-law jacked the old barn up, blocked it with stones, slid two large wooden beams under the foundation, and then lowered the barn on to them. They hitched Uncle Anton's 15 30 to one beam and Dad's 15 30 to the other, put them both into low gear, revved the throttles to full power. At a nod of the head, the clutches were released in unison, and the barn was moving south, pulled by two 15 30 McCormick Deerings side by side.

Other outbuildings, pens, and fences were hastily constructed, livestock moved over, and life began at the new place for everyone. I should say everyone but Mousie, the pregnant cat who was not about to bring her new family into this strange place. So, Mousie walked back to her nest under the foundation of the stone Bullinger house and had her kittens. Marian and I found them and brought them to our new home, fixing a nest in the manger of the barn. But it didn't work. Mousie spent the night transferring them back to the nest at the Bullinger place.

A day later, tragedy struck this cat family. We watched Mousie coming slowly from the north, carrying a baby kitten, which she put into a nest she had fashioned in the corner of the barn in some hay.

Mousie looked roughed up. She smelled of skunk. She started limping northward. Marian and I followed at a distance to see what she was up to. She crawled into a crevice on a rock pile a short distance from the old Bullinger house and retrieved another kitten, carrying it home. Marian and I dug into the rocks and rescued another. Two were dead outside of the old house. Mousie had apparently transferred them all to the rock pile, the crevice being too small for a skunk to get into, and from there, carried them to the barn one at a time.

Three kittens lived, but Mousie never got well and died shortly thereafter. She must have gotten beat up bad by them skunks. So ended the sad story of Mousie, our mother cat.

How to Dig Your Own Well

Water, life-giving water, was one of my father's concerns when he chose the building spot for our new homestead. Nearby was a swampy area about 200 feet across, where neither man nor beast stepped lest they sink as in quicksand. Cattails and other marsh-like plants abounded. Water bubbled up like the oil out of Jed Clampett's place before he moved to Beverly Hills. A "spring" it was called. Lots of water here. It was centrally located between the house and barns and was open year round, which meant it didn't freeze over. A really good asset.

The spring needed to be developed though. A crane-like machine (a dragline) would simplify the development procedure, but none was available in the area. Nor could dad afford it. So, here's the hard way to develop a spring: Shovel in hand, we wade into the center of the mud (slog is a better word, as we are up to our knees in mud and sinking). Now we spend the next several hours scooping out a pit that is 3 feet in diameter and 5 feet deep, down to the coal bed below it.

A high-volume water pump nearby ran constantly, keeping the water out our dig. Then we lowered a steel culvert-like pipe, fitted with a small pipe connection, down to the top of the coal surface over where the water source was bubbling out of the coal fissure. We had captured the water from the spring. Our next step was to create a stock water tank. We dug a ditch leading to the stock water tank and then shoveled the mud back around the exterior of the culvert, where it all eventually dried up, as the water source now was contained inside the culvert. That's the hard way to develop a spring.

The culvert fills up, the stock tank fills up and spills over creating a rivulet, which will flow by the chicken house so the chickens can drink, through the pigs' pasture, who will enjoy it immensely while wallowing in mud, and then flow into a pond in the cows' meadow. Perfect! For domestic use, water will be dipped out of the culvert with buckets and toted up the little hill to the house. Marian and Raymond will go "down the hill to fetch a pail of water." The house was about 50 yards away, up a little slope. With the spring flowing into the culvert, the surrounding area would dry up. An added bonus was an ice-skating rink that developed in the winter. Mission accomplished, we hoped.

Now us spring developers have to clean up. This has been a dirty task. We have mud all over ourselves. The easiest, but not the most comfortable, way to clean up is to strip naked and sit in the stock tank of cold spring water with a brush and soap. Clothes, including shoes, were also washed and wrung out in the stock tank.

Trading up from Henry Ford's Model T

I remember little about our Model T Ford. I kind of remember it being in the sod garage and seeing a picture of mother sitting behind the wheel, although I never saw her drive it or any other motorized unit. The story is that Dad ordered this T from a dealer in Killdeer, North Dakota, which was 18 miles from the farm. When notified of its arrival, Dad made an early morning walk 18 miles to town, took delivery, and drove it home, arriving in mid-afternoon. The early Ts had tarp-like, fabric tops and were retractable, an early version of the convertible. On a nice day passengers could enjoy the view and wave at passing horse-drawn buggies and perhaps some other stalled Ts.

The T was a basic car. Later Dad had finer things in mind. In 1927, he traded the T for a new Essex Super 6 Tudor sedan. Now this was the ultimate auto; ahead of its time. The Essex was remarkable. It was unlike any car we had experienced. It would be our family sedan until 1942. Dad didn't let me drive it until I was 12, unlike the truck, which I drove when I was 10. The International truck, which was purchased in 1928, was the most used machine on the farm. It plowed through muddy and rutted and snow choked roads, trails, and fields. It carried my sisters Marian, Magdalen, and me to church, dances, and parties. I learned to drive at age 10 (more about that next).

Underage Driving

The International truck was an all-around iron workhorse that never complained. The truck, a 1928 International 6 Speed Special, as they were called, arrived in time to haul building material for the new farmstead. The one-ton truck had a 60-bushel box (a bed) on the back, which Dad enlarged by adding another board to increase the height. It had red wheels, black fenders, and a gray cab. But it had no bumpers. Its cargos included grain, coal, fuel, feed, seed, steel, lumber, cattle, pigs, dogs, dirt, stones and rocks, and sand, to name a few. Also it pulled and towed carts, trailers, farm implements, and dead cows and horses into the hog pasture for them to eat. (Yes, I know it's disgusting, but that's how dead animals were disposed of.)

I had been watching Dad drive the truck, shifting the lever from first to second to third while coordinating the clutch pedal with the moves. It looked easy. I would practice this sequence over and over when the truck was parked. "I can drive this; I know it," I thought to myself. And drive it I did. One morning Mom and Dad went to Dickinson with the Essex, leaving Marian and me in charge at home. They would be gone most of the day. It would be a good time to test my driving skills.

The truck had what was called a two-speed axle. Pushing down a lever added 3 more speeds, thus the "6 Speed Special" name. The extra gears were slower but more powerful. Low range. I decided for safety sake this was the way to go for a first time driver. I started the engine, eased the shift lever into reverse, slowly released the clutch, and with a lurch was backing out of the garage. So far, so good. I headed for an open field and did some more practicing. Heck, this was easy and fun.

I drove back to the house, tooted the horn, and invited my siblings on a tour, an invitation they eagerly accepted. After hoisting

This is the truck that was so much a part of my early life. Decades later, it's still running, I'm told, determined to outlast me. It used to be gray, but now it is red. Maybe gray would be more befitting, given how old it is.

Bob, our mutt dog aboard, we were on our way: Out to the pasture, among the cows, tooting the horn, yelling, and Bob barking excitedly, his front feet up on the top edge of the box. He had never seen the cows from this vantage point and seemed confused as to how to handle the situation.

After harassing the cattle, we returned to the farmyard and did the same to the chickens. I drove around lanes in the fields for a while. We all enjoyed a really nice drive on this sunny day. So now it's time to put the truck back into the garage. This phase didn't go too well. I hit some oil drums in front of me, pushing them against the front wall, pushing the garage wall off its foundation. It dented the drums, but there was no damage to the truck. We pushed the truck back into its proper spot and turned the drums with the dented sides to the wall, which we pried and pounded back onto the foundation with bars and sledge hammers. All was well, until someone tattled. But the scolding wasn't too severe. I think Dad kind of expected this stunt and was thankful no one got hurt. From then on, he let me drive.

Once while out hunting, I tried to cross the Knife River, got the truck stuck, and had to get winched out. When I was 13, Dad had me load and haul grain to market in Killdeer. We hauled 60 bushels per load, making two trips daily until we had hauled 1,000 bushels. The truck now lives in Minnesota, and is still running and chugging handsomely down the street in 4th of July parades with my brother Florian at the wheel.

Attending a New School

Prospect No. 1, the name of our new institution of learning, was somewhat over a mile south of the new farmstead. The road was graded, so it was an easy walk, unlike the cow paths we trudged on to get to Fayette No. 1 the year before. There were two schools in the Prospect district, so apparently it had more financial resources. Prospect No. 1 was a well-maintained structure. It had a vestibule where kids could stomp the snow off their boots before they entered the main classroom, a coal room, ample windows for light, a small spinet piano, and of course the traditional potbelly stove with the metal surround.

The school ground was fenced, and there was a horse barn that provided shelter for Paint and Dobbin, who toted in a family of students from the hills to the east. They were hillbillies and kind of seedy, but nice kids. There were no big burley knife-wielding Russian bullies threatening to separate me from my twins. There were, however, three big Germans, but they weren't mean, and one was my cousin Paul, so I felt safe enough.

It wasn't too long until I was one of a group of troublemakers the teachers had to deal with. My first teacher, Miss Scharr, didn't take time to listen to my upside-down-4 crusade either, so I gave up. However, Mrs. Roshau, who taught me 3rd and 4th grade, had a little trouble with us hoodlums. One recess we barricaded the door by propping a plank against it, so she was unable to ring the bell when recess ended. We needed to finish the inning of the game. First things first! I was also mad at her for making me stay after school one time for accidentally taking her son's gloves home by mistake. His were identical to mine. At home I discovered mine deep in my pocket. "He almost froze his little fingers off," she later told me.
I apologized. "Sorry, ma'am."

Miss Wannamacher, who taught grades 5 and 6, was an excellent teacher but nothing exciting happened. She boarded at our house one winter. How we managed that with a house full of kids, I don't remember. Grades 7 and 8: Mr. Jost was my best teacher. But he was a man, so no more shenanigans. He played baseball with us at recess, but when he started for the door, yellin,' "Schooool tiiime," there was no barricading the door, and the result of the uncompleted inning remained unknown. I was amazed to read of Mr. Jost's passing in 2007. I thought he was gone a long time ago. Had I known he was living, I'd have stayed in touch. All the country schools are gone now. Prospect No.1 is now a farm building on a nearby farmstead. Maybe a pig barn.

Edna Wannamacher, my 5th and 6th grade teacher. She boarded at our house her second year teaching at Prospect No. 1. Can you imagine all of us kids and the teacher in such a small house? Somehow, we made do.

My toughest opponent in the classroom was Cousin Elizabeth (Betty), whose passion was to beat me in tests with higher grades. And she usually did. I didn't like her. However, I got even. I passed the state 8th grade exam, and she didn't. Ha, ha, Betty! You had to go back for half a year. You and Jack Roshau both. You two had to take the test over! I also won the district spelling contest and went on to the county competition in Dunn Center, where I met my match. There, I and everyone else got out spelled by this little blonde, Marie Commes. (I had never heard a last name like that. Later I would learn it was a French name.) I was fascinated and fell in love with her (puppy love). I thought maybe someday I would marry her. But I was a month shy of being 14, so I knew I shouldn't be thinking of marrying yet. But I couldn't get her out my mind. And now, 73 years later, she's still on my mind and married to me. How's that for planning ahead? Cousin Elizabeth, I'm not mad at you anymore. I love you now. I wish we could have coffee and visit sometime.

Depression Stories

It is in the early 1930s, and my parents are looking very depressed and worried. They are talking about unpaid taxes and payments on stuff. It hasn't rained for a long time. The last two crops have been so-so, and the prices of wheat and cattle were down. There were now six kids to feed and clothe. Grandpa Carl, sensing the strain on his son, went to the courthouse and paid Dad's taxes to keep us from getting kicked off our farm. And he couldn't very well rant to son George about having kids because he and Grandma had nine.

1933 got worse. Still no rain, no crop, no hay. Only weeds. Russian thistles, mostly huge ones, rolled across dry dusty fields where they had grown, sucking up the bit of moisture of the night dew where wheat, oats, corn, and barley were planted but failing to grow. These monstrous weeds piled up against fences, offering windbreaks for the bone-dry topsoil, and sand blew off of and across the tilled and seeded fields. These pileups created dunes that livestock could walk across, which they did, in search of vegetation for survival in the neighbor's fields. Not a good situation.

The sun was a tan blurb in the sky with all the sand blowing in the air. Some folks who had money in the banks were out of luck when they failed and locked their doors. The lucky folks who withdrew their money before the lockout tucked it "under the mattress," as the saying goes. Others buried their cash in tin cans "ten steps southwest of the house" or "three shovel lengths from the big tree toward the chicken coop." So the stories were told.

No cans were buried under George and Barb's dirt, and there were no lumps in the mattress either, flat busted they were. Milking a few skinny cows for cream to sell and snitching eggs from under the chickens generated a meager cash flow for material to sew dresses for the girls. Cotton flour and sugar sacks provided cloth for undergarments

Mother's down-by-the-spring garden was producing veggies. The sub-moisture and rich lowland soil grew vegetables in abundance. Her canning operation cluttered up the hot kitchen, which was fueled with dry cow chips (poop). Meanwhile we kids were out in the pasture with a wagon gathering more. Others were fetching pails of water from the spring down below the hill. Jars and lids, peeling, dicing and slicing, boiling and cooking, her perspiring and wiping her brow with her apron. Barbara's operation was something to behold. The shelving in the root cellar would need center supports, that's for sure. And maybe more shelves added. We also would have a pile of potatoes in there. The garden by the spring was a godsend. No crop failure ever occurred there. Plants just grew.

1934: Starving Livestock

1934 had to be the worst of the "Dirty Thirties." It was the year that was the most gut wrenching for both Dad and me. Starving livestock. Cows, skin and bone they were. Calves, the same thing. They hardly had the strength to stand and nurse on their mothers. And what was the good of that? They had no milk. Eyes watery and sore, their teeth were worn out from the dust and dirt of trying to graze roots, as the grass above was nonexistent from the relentless drought. Hang on, it has to rain soon.

Clouds built up in the west almost every afternoon, heavy and loaded with life-giving rain, thunderheads forming, lightening flashing, getting closer. "Hail Mary, full of grace, forgive us our sins. Please let it rain." Nothing. Lightening cracked, slicing into the ground, followed instantly by brain-jarring claps of thunder, then a howling windstorm and a few raindrops, but barely enough to settle the dust. Then the storm was gone, moving on to the southeast, toward the Norbys and Johnsons, who were not Catholic and didn't even know the Hail Mary. In fact, they didn't go to any church. Now is this fair?

The storm left in its wake a lightning strike on a fence east of the barn, splintering our fence posts to shreds for a quarter mile. They needed to be repaired first thing in the morning or 40 hungry cows and calves would stampede for freedom.

The weather pattern repeated itself almost every afternoon on hot days, giving people hope and cowmen holding onto herds. "It's going to rain any day now," they figured. It didn't. Besides, there was no market for products. None whatsoever for cattle or hogs. Nowhere to go with them. Well, not quite. Many pig farmers loaded their runty porkers into wagons and trucks and headed for the nearest town, for Main Street, where they parked, dropped the endgate, kicked the squealing porkers out, and hollered "Come get 'em!" to the gathering curious crowd. Kids chased and tried to catch the pigs. The farmers then maybe stopped at Tony's Tavern for a cold beer and visited a little before heading home.

My Dad disposed of his surplus squealers by giving them away at the farm. Residents of Killdeer, (a nearby town) would catch the pigs right out of the pen, a daunting task for a city dude. Families usually brought their kids to do this dirty work, yelling helpful hints and encouragement to them from outside the pens and holding the gates open at the appropriate moments. Dad got "thank yous," but never more. At least the herd was culled and the feed supply lasted longer. The Wetch family was in the butchering business, so they must have gotten a boost from butchering these pigs. "Trickle-down economics" it was for the Wetches.

Selling Starving Cattle to the Government

I am no good at arguing in the political arena but must tell you. Had it not been for the liberal policies of President Franklin Delano Roosevelt (FDR), every farm in the nation would have been lost in another year of drought. Who could survive this onslaught of bad behavior by nature and the economy? It was like the two were working in concert out to destroy us.

So, here we are, sitting on the top corral rail looking down at our cows, calves, and steers, with Mr. Gerht, a neighbor appointed by the U.S. government to put a price on these pathetic cattle. Mr. Gerht walked among them with a can of branding liquid and a sickle section (a triangular piece of steel made out of a hay mower). He used it as a tool, dunking and marking Roman numbers on the right hips of the animals. "XX" equaled $20. This was the top paid for any animal. Calves topped out at "V," not much veal there. Old cows averaged maybe "XII." Baloney bulls "XV."

Louie asked that the herd be delivered to the Killdeer railroad stockyards on a given day. Dad and I looked at one another with the same thought: "Drive these skin and bones 18 miles to Killdeer? No way." But we did, slowly. Calves were hauled on the trucks, which followed the herd.

Along the way we were joined by neighbors also on this trek toward the dreaded destination. It took all day. Government people walked along on the walkway above the stockyard corrals near the railroad, clipboards in hand, tallying the Xs, Vs, and so forth on the scrawny bovine hips below, to be submitted to the U.S. department of who knows what. The check would come in the mailbox later.

These thousands of cattle were not done traveling yet. The worst was yet to come: a train ride to somewhere in the east, a destination unknown to us, and thankfully so. Who cares now? Rumors had it that those with some flesh were slaughtered and canned and distributed as "relief," it was called: relief being another government program to help the hungry. Being on relief was a stigma the proud tough rural survivors avoided. But eventually almost all succumbed to it to some degree, including George and Barbara Schmidt. It was a humbling experience for them to be seen in line at the distribution center set up at the railroad depot but taking solace in the fact that their well-off neighbors were also in the group. "Hi, George. Hi, Barb," they would greet each other sheepishly.

Meanwhile, somewhere 50 miles east, a bulldozer operator sat, engine idling, smoking a cigarette, waiting and watching for riflemen walking along the top of the huge pit he had gouged out of the dry dirt to finish using their marksmanship skills on the worthless cattle we and others had sold to the government. Afterward, he'd get to restoring the topsoil to its original grade, but a bit higher, rounded on top and like a huge grave.

Government "Relief"

In Killdeer, as in other towns, large and small, relief distribution stations were set up, usually at or near train depots. "Commodities" and "relief" this stuff was called. They included fresh fruits, mostly apples and oranges, canned meats (our cows?), and canned veggies and fruits all in gallon cans printed with the words "NOT TO BE SOLD." There were 50-lbs. bags of flour and cereals such as oatmeal and wheat meal. Some Fridays there were also potatoes and turnips.

Later, as the recession dragged on, children's clothes were added to the list. When kids from the poorest families came to school wearing fancy duds, they were heckled and harassed by their ragged classmates. Distribution day was Friday because the train with the provisions came in Thursday evening.

To be eligible for assistance, families needed to fill out an application form. Then a committee of local citizens would visit the homes, look over the situation, and make a decision as to whether or not the assistance was really needed. Folks had to be destitute to get it. The most destitute family in our neighborhood was nearly starving but was not eligible for assistance because they didn't owe any money on their small farm. You had to have debts to qualify. Mrs. Little went to the board and raised hell and got them some help.

Another family had no car, so they drove a mismatched team of horses (one small and one very large horse that limped) hitched to a rickety two-wheeled cart 18 miles to Killdeer and back every Friday, rain or shine. They started early and came home late. They failed at farming and eventually moved to town and lived on welfare. My parents got kicked off relief because someone reported we were putting up a building. This disqualified them. We were building a coal shed out of old boards from the former Bullinger henhouse roof. My Uncle Florian got four sacks of spuds taken away by the county sheriff because he had bought a new mower or something.

So that's how it was in the Dirty Thirties, with Mother Nature being the major contributing factor. But today we read about 47 million U.S. citizens living in poverty. What's the reason for this? You can't blame the weather this time.

There are those who attribute poverty to laziness and poor education, which may be true to some extent. But there are many other reasons for poverty beyond people's control, Illnesses, disabilities, accidents, injuries, bad money management, and probably the worst demon in this hellfire is alcohol, the most dangerous drug by far.

I think most people would like to be working at a job they enjoyed. Neither political party has come forth with a solution to help these people live the American Dream. "The poor will always be with us," the saying goes. I wish it weren't so. It is hard to watch.

My Disastrous Rain and Fire Incident

This is an embarrassing incident in my life. I wasn't going to mention it, but many of my family members have heard of it, so I better explain. In 1935, I burned down a wheat field. It rained that spring.

"Beautiful, beautiful! Thank you, Holy Mary, Mother of God. We thought you had forsaken us; forgotten us peasants out here on this Russian-thistle-infested dusty prairie, where the sand dunes now covered the fences like snowdrifts in the winter, reminders of the awful days that created them."

Now rain. (This is just a teaser. Mary would be sending us more penance for our sins or whatever the reason. A heat wave perhaps?) The country is basking in incredible greenery for the first time in years, and grass is tall in the cow pasture, not that there is any good in that. The cows are no longer in need of grass where they are in Beulah.

But this is fine. Great! We have lots of hay on the school section. The wheat crop will be bountiful, and the price per bushel was up 25 cents over it was in 1934. We will buy new cows. Some well-off folks who go to our church, St. Edward's, are buying new Plymouths and Chevies. But not George Schmidt. He is driving the Essex. "Assaches!" the well-off folks heckled us, when it was parked among their new models on Sunday at 10 o'clock Mass.

The pasture and range land would recover from years of overgrazing, and the topsoil rebuilt. All was well. Then, one Sunday in early in July, disaster: A 30-plus mph wind with 105 temperatures destroyed everything in its path. The wheat, 30-inches tall, was headed out, but not a kernel of grain was in them yet. By evening, the green had turned yellow. Fields of dried-up stubble, we had. Useless stubble. It was fertile ground for a new crop of weeds and tumbleweeds. Mr. Schmidt wouldn't be selling any wheat or stopping by the courthouse to pay taxes when the work was done in the fall.

I asked Dad what he planned to do with these fields of sticks, and he replied, "burn them, I guess." Burning trashy fields and ditches and weedy areas always was his favorite form of weed control. "Burning up the seeds," as he put it. So one day while working in the area, I decided to help him out. I didn't like weeds any better than he did, especially Russian thistles.

The blaze consumed about 15 acres and also destroyed some barley shocks (small stacks of 8-10 bundles cut and stacked and awaiting threshing). Alarmed neighbors came to assist. Burning was common, but this one was out of season. I was sorry and ashamed. In fact, I feel kind of sorry and ashamed now, so let's go on to another story.

FROM THE FARM TO FAST FOOD

Completing My Education—in the 8th Grade

It is 1936. I am 14 and have 8 years of education in my head. Where to from here? High school is 20 miles away in Killdeer. It might as well be on the moon. There is no way I can go. Dad is bent over with *lumbago*, as it was called (a backache). He needs help, and farmers didn't raise sons to sit in high schools. There is serious farming to be done here. High school is for girls so they can be secretaries in offices until they get married.

So now I am full-time farmer. I already know how to operate all the equipment and machines. Heavy plowing, tilling, and seeding were done with tractor power; harrowing, haying, and harvesting were done with horse power (a team- of four-horses). It was hard work. Rounding the horses up every morning became almost impossible. They didn't cooperate, as they knew what was coming: pulling a heavy hunk of iron and a guy sitting behind you with a whip ready to whop you across the rump if you slow down a little. That's what's coming.

Working with horses was time consuming. They had to get curried, grained, watered, harnessed, hitched up, and worked till noon. Unhitch, water, grain, and give them hay before I have lunch. Then hitch them up again. Work them till sundown, unharness, curry and grain them again, and then turn them into the pasture at night. Day after day, repeat the above. Except Sunday.

Mass was at 10 A.M. at St. Edward's Church, five miles north. Confession and communion were necessary, according to my mother. She probably heard sinful profanity coming from the horse barn during the week and would rather see her son Raymond in heaven than hell. To receive the sacrament of communion, one must fast from midnight on. Then you must stand in line with other sinners going to confession before Mass. I had a standard, one-size-fits-all confession with occasional variations memorized so the priest wouldn't get suspicious. By the time we got home, the pan-fried chicken, mashed potatoes, and gravy tasted good, even though my mother wasn't the best cook.

There was an incident when I was sure I was destined for eternal hell, and it haunted me. Forgetting I was going to communion, one Sunday morning I ate a little peppermint out of a jar sitting on a dresser. Eating anything before communion was a mortal sin (mortal being the deadliest of the sin group). Doomed to suffer in hell forever, I was to be. Maybe I still am?

Scared Straight: My Religious Upbringing

St. Edward's Church, a once impressive structure, was built in 1923 by the immigrant German-Russian farmers in the area. But today St. Edward's is no more. It was hauled away to become a cattle loafing shed, perhaps.

Religion, of course, was a vital component in our upbringing. It perhaps had the most profound effect on our lives. My mother was deeply religious and constantly preached the horrors of committing sin. Her description of hell was so horrific it was unimaginable. The worst part was that there was no end. The doomed would be in hell forever. Now a child hearing this from his or her mother would be inclined to turn out good, I would think.

Every summer for two weeks following the end of the school year, we kids were hauled to St. Edward's for "summer school" to learn the catechism, a book of the Catholic religion's doctrine. Almost all the kids in the parish attended except perhaps the older boys, who were helping to put in crops, which trumped catechism.

The teacher was Rev. Kirchenbichler, a German. He was our parish priest then, and drove his Model A Ford 40 miles to and from Dickinson every day and Sunday. The Rev. Kirchenbichler used a pointer, a stick with a little ball on the end, for charts and maps, etc. He also used it for whacking us kids on the noggin' when we showed boredom with his teaching style or were disruptive. Strict, he was!

Rev. Kirchenbichler also reiterated my mother's warnings of the dangers of sinning. So, I was getting a double whammy, which was enough to take the sin issue quite seriously. There were two classes of sins: venial and mortal, the latter being the most deadly. Mortal sins included the worst stuff like murder and the most worrisome, immorality: Running off with your neighbor's wife, extra-marital sex, premarital sex, immodest thoughts or actions (that's a tough one, Reverend), and stuff like that. "Mortal sins are not forgivable," Rev. Kirchenbichler said. This worried me.

Venial sins like sticking your tongue out at your sister or mother were no big deal. A penance of saying Catholic prayers ("Our Fathers" and "Hail Marys") took care of that, providing you were sincere about your promise not to do it again. But mortal sin was a sentence to hell. It was enough to keep me a gentleman when out on dates with girls, but I still worry about the peppermint thing.

Shooting and Selling Rabbits in 1936: You Have to Make Money Somehow

The winter of 1935-36 was very, very cold. There were lots of jackrabbits. The thermometer was stuck below zero for 70 days and nights. Dad hauled us to and from Prospect No. 1 in a straw-bedded bobsled, with Prince and Charlie doing the pulling, trotting briskly with their nostrils flared. Dad was clapping his hand together in an effort to avert frostbite. Meanwhile I, with my .22 single-shot Winchester, was shooting at jackrabbits, which were everywhere along the roadside wherever vegetation showed above the snow in the ditches. I didn't get very many from a moving sled while having numb, cold hands. Dad wouldn't stop to pick them up on the trip to school but reluctantly did so on the evening trip home. Meanwhile, my sisters whined and complained from under the quilts where they snuggled to try to keep unfrozen.

But rabbits worth 50 cents each at Dickinson Hide & Fur were worth stopping for, I would think. The jacks were numerous that winter. I would set a dozen traps around the haystack in the evening and have rabbits in all of them in the morning. Dad was having a rough year. But at age 13, I was having a windfall selling rabbits.

1936 brought the end of my educating, with state exams, spelling bees, athletic meets, etc. I passed the state exams, won a regional spelling meet, and, as I have explained before, went on to the Dunn County competition, where I and everyone else were trounced by a diminutive, pert blonde from the Germania district, wherever that was. I saw her again at the graduation ceremony at a community hall and picnic a week later. She was an 8th grade graduate as was I. I watched her from a distance. Today it would be called stalking, I suppose. I was too bashful to walk over and introduce myself. I was worried she may be from a rich family (high-class folks) and would turn up her nose at me and tell me to get lost. No, better to wait and find out more about her.

So now I am fully educated, an 8th grade graduate. Where to now? Dad has a bad back and needs help. I want to be an aviator or house builder but for sure not a farmer. Heaven forbid! A musician? That's it. I could learn that at home, and when I was 21, I'd be an adult with rights. And I would leave this farm and become a famous accordionist and find and marry Marie Commes.

1937: The Attack of the of the Grasshoppers

The hoppers flew in one summer day. Clouds of them. It was like the sun had lost its power to shine. Where did them pests come from? It remains a mystery to me that scientists and agronomists or any kind of "ists" didn't or couldn't see this disaster coming. Maybe it was because in those days they had no radar. I don't know how large an area these characters attacked, but the whacked the county real good. They were big and hungry, very hungry, taking to chewing up even hardwood tool handles and the siding of buildings. It was near harvest time, and the grain was ripening and almost ready for cutting. But the greedy bugs were hanging on every plant and chewing and biting off the wheat heads, which fell to the ground, lost.

The U.S. government sprung into action to help. It made available free sacks of poisoned bran to be spread on the fields in an effort to eradicate these pests. Innovative mechanics and blacksmiths and welders joined the fight by utilizing junked rear wheels axles\and drive shafts of cars. The blacksmiths and welders made them into primitive spreaders, much like today's lawn spreaders.

Before the coming of these mechanical spreaders, Mom and Dad sat in the wagon facing backward with a sack of the hopper Happy Meal between them. They tossed the poison out like they were feeding chickens while I drove the wagon back and forth across the fields littered with wheat heads. Hordes of hungry hoppers took flight to get out of our way. But the poison also killed birds, which also munched this concoction. Another hazard was farm animals eating it. All things considered, it was a disaster, but worth a try.

On windy days Dad and I would hitch up two teams to wagons and put a long wire between us. Going downwind we would strafe the field hoping to get them hoppers airborne so they would fly to another planet. This wasn't very effective either. The roadways were slick with dead hoppers, and the radiators on tractors and vehicles were plugged with them. Walking in a field created a swooshing noise as hordes of them took flight in front of you. When they finished eating us out of house and home, they took flight and were gone.

So another crop was lost. Another year of wasted work and resources. That meant more worrying about surviving. Land payments were not too big a problem. The mortgage holders would have no buyers for farms anyway. For 50 cents an acre you could buy the whole county. But who would want a farm? By summer's end, the hopper population plague had abated, and a severe cold winter followed, apparently destroying the eggs. So, in the year 1938, the hopper infestation was minimal.

Battling Monster Tumbleweeds on the Prairie

The one thing that grew well in the drought years was Russian thistles (tumbleweeds). Well maybe I shouldn't cuss them as they might have been many a cattleman's salvation. Brought to the U.S. by Russian immigrants in contaminated seed sacks and a variety of other containers, the prickly tumbleweeds spread quickly. Growing up to 5 ft. in diameter, they danced and bounced happily along in the wind, scattering seeds with every hop, stopped only by a barbwire fence or the bumper of a passing Model A Ford as they bounded out of the ditch to cross the road, only to be dragged 50 or so yards before getting loose and resuming the trip into the neighbor's field. The neighbor had no grounds for complaint because his tumbleweeds were spreading seed of their own, likely into the next township. These nasty suckers each had thousands thorns, stickers, barbs, or whatever you want to call them. They would get up your pant legs, under your collar, and into other places. A real pain in the you know what, they were, and a reminder of other Russian problems in my life. (I kind of liked a Russian girl named Sana for a little while. But in those days, Germans were not supposed to "go steady" with Russians, so Sana was "off limits.")

Deeper rooted thistles that stayed in the field needed to be removed before tilling could be done. Ingenious methods were devised to do this, burning being the favorite, if the stand of thistles was thick. However, a fire break had to be plowed around them first. We raked them into piles with a horse-drawn hay rake and then burned them or in my case, drug a harrow across them with the International one windy day when Dad was in Dickinson with the Essex.

Agronomists came to the rescue. They discovered that early-stage thistles were quite nutritious for cattle, so we began harvesting them like hay and blending them with drought-damaged grain straw. The mix becomes palatable winter cow chow. But the thistles also needed to be cut and staked at the right time before they dried in the field.

Enter my sister Marian. Welcome to the thistle field. I mowed and raked, and together we hauled and stacked the thistles. She was on the stack, shaping it, and I pitching it up to her. The stuff was heavy with moisture, so the work got harder as the stacks grew in height. From whatever source these prickly obnoxious weeds derived moisture to grow in the bone dry dirt was a mystery to me. As the thistles dried, they turned black. "Guess what's fer supper, Bessie? Black thistle hay! Ya think you can ruminate this stuff around and turn it into a bucket of milk?"

Getting "Drafted" into the Civilian Conservation Corps (CCC)

The Schmidts have been hammered by drought, scorching temps, grasshoppers, and low prices for the few bushels of wheat and cattle they have had to sell. A total gross income $840 for 1937. George and Barbara are about out of the agriculture business, as is most everyone else in the area. Enter FDR, who implemented the WPA, or Works Progress Administration. (That's an impressive name, don't you think? Who wouldn't want to work for an organization like that?) The WPA was made up of men building roads with shovels instead of graders and dozers. It was inefficient but earned a man $40 a month ($48 if you furnished a team of horses to pull Fresnos, a mini dirt hauler). Dad signed up for six months, October through March. The project involved cutting down a hill and eliminating a curve in the road three-quarter miles south of the farm, so it was near home.

The Civilian Conservation Corp (CCC), another government program, would be my habitat for the same six months. The CCC was for 18-to-28 year olds. I was 17, but nobody bothered to check. I and several other enlistees were stationed at North Roosevelt Park. North and South Roosevelt Parks are national parks named after President Teddy Roosevelt, who spent a total of two years in the area going broke in cattle ranching. Building the park would be our project: scenic roads, trails, observation towers, picnic areas, etc.

At North Roosevelt Park, we joined 200 other young guys who had enlisted as well. The CCC camps had a military flavor. We were issued uniforms and assigned barracks, of which there were twenty. There were army style drills, assemblies, and standing- at-attention, inspections, while a mean-looking Looie (lieutenant) slowly walked by, glaring at us rookies, checking to see if the seams in our khaki shirts and pants were ironed straight, our shoes were shined, and our black ties were clean. He was running a first-class operation here. You rookies get that fact through your heads! Better learn this right away!

Another character was Master Sarg "Bilko," we called him (when he couldn't hear us). He was like the twin of Sarg in the cartoon strip *Beetle Bailey*. "HHHENSHAH [attention]!" he would bark when entering the barracks with the Looie for his weekly glare at the quality of our housekeeping skills; floors mopped, coal bucket full, and bunks made up correctly the way we were taught. This inspection was usually skillfully executed by the second lieutenant, Looie 2, who was working his way up the CCC food chain.

Oh, and we can't forget the company doctor. He was a military doc. In addition to caring for the general health of 250 CCC-ers, there was one important monthly exam called the "short-arm inspection." The CCC doc would sit on a low stool in the "hospital," a room with several beds where the ill, or those pretending to be ill (especially on cold miserable days when building park roads was not to their liking) lay. Then, 200-plus guys were ordered to get in a line, which moved along at a fair clip.

Getting close to the doc, we would lower our pants and/or long johns. "Skin 'er back," he ordered. Then he peered, looking at pete and the twins, turning them every which way searching for signs of venereal disease (VD). Quite frequently a guy in front would yell, "Ouch!" and do a little jump, an indication that pete was pointing too far north for proper examination, which the doc remedied with an effective thumb and forefinger flick. At one inspection, Eddie, a diminutive five-foot-tall guy, startled the doc. "Holy buckets!" he yelled, staring at Eddies attributes. "I've seen dongs on guys, but never visa-versa. This is amazing!" Little Eddie became the envy of the camp. Nobody picked on him anymore.

VD was a concern because every Saturday a camp truck would go to Watford City, which was about 20 miles north. The truck was like an army troop carrier with a bench seat on both sides and a tarp over the roof. We could check out of camp and ride the truck to town if we wanted to. There was usually a dance, and some guys had relationships with girls. "Going steady" it was called back then. The truck returned at 1 or 2 A.M. but not always with all aboard. Those missing found other means of getting back to camp.

The food in the Cs was good. Better than I would have eaten at home, but complaining was going on. "The hell with you," Cookie snarled at the enlistees. "You'll eat what I serve and shut up." Cookie was a master sergeant with a John Wayne attitude; he didn't take "no" from nobody. He had a standard menu that repeated itself every week. "Slumbullion" beef stew on Monday, and "s--t on shingles" on Tuesday, which utilized Monday's leftovers; these are two dishes that I remember.

All of us privates "got drafted" for kitchen duty. I always enjoyed my week of being Cookie's "slave," though. *While you are resting* was his favorite phrase. "Schmitty, while you are resting, do you have time to fetch me a couple of no. 10 cans of peaches out of the storeroom, please?" There was a mountain of spuds to peel, dishes to wash, and lots of other stuff to do "while you were resting." Working out in the field meant shoveling dirt and wheeling it to its destination. It also meant drilling and blasting stone for the rock-quarry guys to chisel into various shapes required for the park entrance and visitors' lookouts. We also mined and loading scoria, a light, heavily pitted volcanic rock. More about mining scoria shortly. . .

This is the "main street" of the CCC camp. The barracks are the buildings on the sides of the picture, and building on the far end was the latrine, where we went to shower, wash up, pee, and poop. Imagine a row of 50 guys sitting on an outhouse-style facility doing their daily thing, casually reading and grunting, while others are snarling at them to hurry it up. Nearby, others are shaving and showering.

MORE CCC STORIES

The woodworking shop at the camp was my favorite hangout for spending evenings. It was spacious, well lit, and full of tools and machines, the likes of which I didn't know existed. These were industrial quality machines. The woodworking instructor, Mr. Kulish, taught me a lot. The surrounding badlands afforded an ample supply of red aromatic cedar logs, which we converted into chests to take home for our mothers' Christmas presents. Mr. Kulish, family lived in Dickinson, 60 miles distant, and he would go home almost every weekend, weather and roads permitting. Driving his Model A Ford sedan, he financed the trip by taking passengers for 25 cents roundtrip. The car had capacity of six at the most, so we sat on each other's laps. For 15 cents you could ride on the outside, standing on the running board and hang onto the door handle. This was not recommended in cold weather for a 60-mile trip. Mr. Kulish didn't sell too many 15 cent rides. I went to Dickinson often with my cousin Tony, who was also a CCCer with me. This is a heart-wrenching story. I went with Tony to visit his sister, age 5, who was hospitalized following a ruptured appendix. She wasted away to a skeleton before passing months later. It was hard to watch and a humbling experience that taught me of the fragility of life.

While on the fragility-of-life subject, back to the scoria pit: Seven of us shovelers were loading trucks in the pit, creating an overhanging large hunk of frozen earth above. The foreman came by and ordered us the hell out of there "before that thing breaks loose and kills someone!" It did, the moment he said those words. Tragically, but mercifully, the person's death was instantaneous. Our CCC group went into a shock mode after that. Investigators swarmed all over the place for a month. Now I had seen death twice, the other one being a young Indian rodeo rider bucked off and trampled by a bronc during a blinding rain, lightning, and hail storm at a rodeo one July 4th.

When my six-month stint was up, I and several others were shipped home. My home was only 40 miles south of the camp. However, instead of going straight there, I and others were first trucked to Watford City, N.D., put on a train miles across the border into Montana, where our railcar was uncoupled and pushed onto a siding for a day and a night. Some ex-CCCers utilized this time by getting drunk in the towns. We were then railed back to the east to Dickinson and finally to Killdeer, a total distance of almost 400 miles. I had contributed $25 a month, or $150 total, to my family's income to help pay for tractor fuel and seed for another season of trying to make a living on our farm.

In the later 1930s, conditions improved for farmers. Cattle herds were rebuilt, prices were up, and the soil was getting fertilized after having been blown to kingdom come during the worst of the dust storms. FDR got seed-and-feed loan programs in place. Farmers' Union stations were extending credit for tractor fuel to customers, so optimism returned to rural America. Papa George would be able to pay his real estate taxes and keep his farm.

A Dog Named Bob

One day, Harry Walker, a farmer who lived four miles southwest, drove into our yard in his Model A Ford to talk to Dad about a fence or something. Sitting in the passenger's seat beside him was a black and white dog. It looked like a border collie. Mr. Walker stopped the car and opened the door carefully so as not to let the dog out. But he was too slow. The dog zipped past him and introduced himself by licking the faces of my three siblings, who were playing in the dirt nearby. A kids-loving dog he seemed to be. The Walkers had a son who was grown up and had left home. "The dog's name is Bob," said Mr. Walker. When the two men finished chatting, Mr. Walker called, "Come on Bob. Let's go. C'mon, c'mon, let's go." No response. So, Mr. Walker picked up the reluctant pooch, tucked him on the car's seat, waved goodbye and drove home.

Two hours later Bob was back at our house cozying up to the Schmidt kids again. He was a bit winded from the four-mile trot, but happy. Dad didn't think Bob's deserting his master was a good idea, so he put him in the International and trucked him back home. Mr. Walker thanked him and also speculated that Bob may become a permanent resident of the Schmidt house because keeping him home now would be almost impossible. "I'll lock him up overnight, but if he comes back to your place again, keep him. He'll be yours," he said.

Sure enough, the next day he trotted in, and we owned a bobtailed dog named Bob. I took Bob with me to the pasture to get the milk cows and found him to be a well-trained, cattle-working pooch. He seemed to enjoy this activity. I was happy. A good cow dog is a valuable helper when handling livestock. Bob was always with me when I worked in the fields. He caught rodents and reptiles, chased jackrabbits, and got a nose full of porcupine quills now and then. He never learned a lesson to stay away from those creatures.

But Bob did not go hunting with me. He didn't like guns and would hide when he saw me with one. Perhaps he had been shot at some time in his life of wandering and meandering. Bob was also a playmate of my younger siblings as well as my faithful companion and assistant cowpuncher for years. Eventually he became old and very ill. I fixed him a bed of hay in the barn manger. He was getting worse and was dying. Bob didn't like guns, but I did what I had to do (with a gun) so he wouldn't suffer anymore. So sorry, old friend.

FROM THE FARM TO FAST FOOD

AMERICAN INGENUITY AT WORK

One very windy spring day in 1935, my parents prepared to go to town. Dad outlined my agenda for the day's work: "Hitch up the horses to the harrow, and strafe plow the southwest field, thirty acres, loosening up the thistles so they will roll away (hopefully into the next county) to clear the field for spring plowing," he said.

Walking behind the harrow and four horses, stepping over ten thousand thistles, back and forth, was nothing to look forward to. Thirty acres would take all day, maybe more. I would then have to unhitch and feed and rest the team and eat lunch at noon, which may or may not be ready, as two of my sisters were into listening to soap operas on the battery-powered radio. They were happy to run down the battery when the folks weren't home. *Ma Perkins* and *Pepper Young's Family* were their favorite soaps and aired around noon. This often preempted their fixing my lunch.

After lunch I would have to hitch up again and get back behind those damn thistles and four nags. Not the kind of day a 13-year-old kid looked forward to. There must be a better way. Ah, the powerful International truck. The lowest gear would be about right. Those tumbleweeds would be outta there pronto. And so they were three hours later. It was an easy pull for that International. It pulled the harrows with ease, and I was riding in comfort in the cab instead of walking all day.

The horses were happy, I supposed, but what would Dad say? My sisters would surely tattle on me. (Then again, maybe not. It could backfire on them. I had leverage due to the forbidden radio-listening thing.) But it didn't happen. When Dad came home he peered at the thistle-cleared field in disbelief and mumbled something about getting started on the plowing tomorrow.

My dad and I had a distance between us. It was a sort of strange father-son relationship. He seldom criticized my work but never complimented or praised it either. Mom was often the go-between if communication was necessary. I guess this is how it was between him and his Dad as well. But our relationship slowly improved, and by the time I was 20 years old, it was quite normal.

I also used the International for social events as well. I went to dances at nearby communities with it. Dad was reluctant to let me have the Essex for these junkets, or so Mom told me. So I respected his wish to protect his car and traveled by truck. It was embarrassing sort of, as most of my friends kind of sneered at me, driving to a dance with a farm truck. My sisters who often went with me were even more humiliated. I needed to make some money to buy my own car. The sooner, the better.

"Water Witching" and Well Digging

The Schmidt farmhouse, which was built in 1928, is shown here. It is now abandoned. Note the little shed on the side. The well we dug is inside of it.

After years of packing hundreds of buckets of water up the path from the spring below, often in inclement weather through mud and snow and suffering numerous tumbles, thought was given to digging a well near the south-side door of the house. We would then build an addition covering it, thereby having a water source without having to step outside. This would be almost sinfully convenient.

Dad speculated that at about thirty feet depth we would tap into the same aquifer feeding the nearby spring. Mr. Hutmacher, a neighbor gifted with the power of "water witching," was summoned. Water witchers walk over an area while grasping a willow stick held horizontally. If the gifted witcher walks over an underground water source, the end of the stick will turn and point downward as though it's magnetic. The willow's sudden dip downward at the very spot of the proposed well site indicated much water. Amazing! Mr.

Hutmacher's witching fee was kind of steep, as he owed Dad for custom feed grinding. This sorta evened things out.

A 38-inch circle was scratched in the dirt, marking the dig site. Equipment consisting of a wheelbarrow, a hand posthole digger, a bucket, a shovel, a rope, and a string-plumb bob was moved in. The excavated soil was to be wheeled and dumped into a nearby ravine. The posthole operator (me) filled the bucket with a rope attached. Dad and my brother Florian pulled it up, dumped it into the wheelbarrow, and lowered the empty pail down to me for refill. And so it went.

As the hole got deeper, a plumb line was centered, assuring a "straight down" hole. Water and solid coal was discovered at 24 feet. So that was the end of the dig. The project took several days. I was hoisted up and down with a rope by Dad and Florian. It was an eerie feeling, being down in that deep hole. No thought was given to the possibility of a cave-in, although it wasn't likely as the soil formation was very firm.

Now came the task of lowering the "casing." The casing would be a galvanized, corrugated-steel, 36-inch, 24-foot-long culvert Dad had bought from somewhere. It came in three 8 ft. sections with connection rings. This simplified the job. But the well was not a huge success. The water vein was not the spring. It was not clear water but kind of rust-colored. It was OK for washing dishes and mopping floors, but for drinking, cooking, and laundry, the spring water was preferred, so going down the hill to fetch a pail of water was not entirely eliminated. The handy pump outside the door wasn't used as much as we had hoped. The shed was later built, which was useful in other ways besides housing a well and pump. We removed our messy overshoes in there before going in the house. Mom liked that.

From Horses to Horsepower

Horses are magnificent animals. They are beautiful, smart and useful. But some are lazy and mean. Lady and Dolly fall into this category. From age 10 to 20, I had horses in my life every day, hitching them up to something, or riding one. I've been kicked, bitten, bucked off, squished, and pooped and peed on. Whatever a horse can do to humans has been done to me. I had reasons to dislike them, and I'll tell you a few that stand out in my mind: Prince and Charlie were a team of well-matched geldings (neutered males). Not large, but lean and muscular, gentle, and well broke. But they seemed to communicate with another and conspire against me. In wintertime, every day I hitched them to the bobsled, backed it up to the barn, cleaned it, and spread the manure onto a field, and then went to a nearby straw stack for a load of straw. I parked the sled up against the stack, and as I climbed up on it, Prince and Charlie took advantage of this interval to gallop back to the barn with the sled. I had to walk home.

Another incident: They ran away hitched to the hay rake out in the field when I got off it to get myself a drink of water from the nearby spring. They were probably angry because they didn't get a drink. This rake escapade didn't end well, however. The open corral gate they galloped through was 8 feet wide and the rake was 10 feet. Well, we needed a new rake anyway. Dad found a nice one for $20.

Dolly, the pony I rode bareback for short rides like fetching milk cows, bucked me off into a cactus patch a mile from home, a painful walk back. Another time she dumped me into a muddy creek. Another painful walk home. I was covered with mud head to foot. Prince and Charlie liked to squish me when I stepped between them in the barn to harness them up. Buck, a big sorrel I rode when doing serious cowboying, fell, rolling over me. Luckily, there was snow under me or I'd have been flattened like a pancake. Lady, a lazy white mare in a four-horse hitch pulling the binder (a harvesting machine), figured out how to eliminate her share of the load, by slowing down to where there was slack in her tugs.

A near disaster with horses almost happened when a sudden lightening storm came up: I was in a field pulling a binder, the horses at a gallop, racing for home. Lightning struck behind me, I felt the heat, but we did make it home before the downpour. Getting bits into a horse's mouth in below zero mornings was also a challenge. The bits would freeze onto their tongues. So we pre-warmed them by dunking the bits into the water tank. Now I like horses. They are beautiful intelligent animals. And I own 180 of them. They are stabled under the hood of my pickup.

The View from the Top of Teepee Butte

When I was a kid, my most favorite place on God's green earth was the top of Teepee Butte. This was a geographical landmark and on Dad's land. The butte was a hill higher than others in the area. It was topped with a huge stone formation, flat on top, and had fissures that created caves to crawl in around and explore. There were names with dates and drawings scratched and carved into the stones. I remember one name in beautiful scroll deep in a little cave. It may be there still. Many names and dates could be found. I should have taken pictures of all this, but at the time it didn't seem important.

"Ray C. Schmidt 1940" boldly carved in stone on the top of Teepee Butte to be there for a century, unless this rock tumbles down the hillside, as many have.

Today, some archeologists might consider the butte to be some sort of historic treasure. It would perhaps be a good idea for someone to go up there with a camera and look to see if anything is left. Looking at recent photos of Teepee Butte shows many of these stone formations have succumbed to the ravages of time and tumbled down the hillside.

This cool dude in the boots next to me is Sabbie (Sebastian) Mischel, the son of my mother's cousin. Sabbie did the driving for his parents when they came to our house for their annual visit. A long 60 mile trip it was in them days. To entertain Sabbie while our parents chatted and drank homemade beer, I took him up Teepee Butte. We spent several hours target shooting at rocks. (Wild game was out of season at the time.).

I spent many Sunday afternoons up there on Teepee Butte. After coming home from church and having lunch, if the day was a clear, I took my telescope and hiked up to the top. I felt so happy it was ours. I would take my friends up there when they came to visit. The view in every direction was so sweeping: I could see Manning, a village 10 miles east, and almost to Killdeer, another burg to the north. Westward, the horizon was at 13 miles.

Fayette was right in front of my nose as I looked through the telescope lens. I watched Mrs. Little, who owned the store at Fayette, and her loyal employee Annie get into Mrs. Little's beautiful streamlined 1934 Ford V8 sedan and drive south east to the Karstens' place, wondering what the heck they wanted to visit them for, given that the Karstens were first-generation German immigrants and could hardly speak English. It didn't make sense to me at all. (The car's chrome wire wheels glinted in the sun. It was kinda neat at the time.)

I watched cars on a nearby highway and utilized the butte's attributes to its fullest extent. My last summer up there was spent carving and chiseling "RAY C. SCHMIDT 1940" into the east face of a stone really deep, so if I ever became famous, the world would come to look. It would be great if it were possible to make one last trek up the side of old Teepee and scan the horizon 360 degrees. I would probably see things differently today. No "streamlined" V8s for sure.

Sneaking a Smoke on a Lunch Break

Back in the mid-thirties, Dad and Chris Hartman leased some acres of "school land" from the state. This was native prairie with a good growth of grass to be cut for hay. I was mowing on the west half, and Ralph Hartman on the east. It was a hard pull for two horses. The grass was thick and tough. It was a slow go, so we packed a lunch. A small grove of trees provided a shady spot for us mower operators and the four horses for the midday much-needed respite. Well, for three horses anyway. You see, Ralph and I decided a relaxing smoke would be nice after bouncing up and down in the damn steel mower seat. But the nearest, "roll your own" makin's were at the Fayette Mercantile, about a mile-and-a-half away. So we interrupted Dobbins' oat munching, swung aboard, and headed for the Mercantile. Finances were meager. We had three nickels between the two of us. It was 5 cents for a sack of Bull Durham, 5 for a Mars bar, and 5 for Nehi Orange Crush. We tied Dobbin to the hitching rail and went inside. Oh boy. Annie Fisher was on duty. Not good. We had hoped for my sister Marian, who worked there at the time.

"One Bull Durham, one Mars, and one Orange Crush, please," I ordered, as Ralph cowered behind me.

"Bull Durham?" asked Annie.

"Yes. It's for my Dad. Dad sent me." Annie glared her famous glare. She knew full well I was lying through my teeth. Dad smoked Velvet tobacco. But she got our order, glaring at us two 14-year old "roll your own" Bull Durham smokers.

"Does Dad need matches, too?" she asked with a bit of sarcasm.

I paid her the 15 cents while trying not to make eye contact with her. The transaction certainly would reach my mother's ears on her next egg-trading visit to the Fayette Mercantile, and from her to Dad. I should have thought of that. Oh well, too late now. Will have to deal with this later.

We led Dobbin to Fayette's well-used water shed tank where she drank her fill as Ralph and I shared and enjoyed the sweet of the Mars and sipped on the Nehi. We could have returned the glass bottle for a penny refund but decided not to. Confronting Annie once was enough. So, we rolled and lit up, climbed aboard Dobbin, and headed southeast, across the bridge, puffing and coughing and "enjoying" our after-lunch smoke. Our sack of Bull Durham lasted quite a while. Annie never tattled to mother that I know of. Bless her heart.

Hooked on Music

A defining hour of my life was the seeing and hearing my friend Jack's brother, play the piano accordion at the 1930 Christmas program at Prospect School No 1. There it was, a beautiful full-sized instrument, with a 41-key piano keyboard on the right and 120 bass buttons on the left. Rhinestones glittered on the ornate grill; it was an awesome sight for this 8-year-old kid to behold. And that sound, that gorgeous sweet music, resonated throughout my body and soul like a refreshing tonic. I had never heard music I liked this well. I had to learn to play this instrument.

Our living room had a pump organ, which mother played, and she had taught me some simple tunes, so I was somewhat familiar with the piano keyboard. I nagged my parents for an accordion. They ordered a buttonbox from Sears. I hated it. Buttonboxes are like harmonicas. You get two notes from the same button, one by pulling and then another by pushing.

Anton Hartman played a buttonbox at namesday parties, these being excuses to tap a keg and celebrate someone's name or something like that. For example: St Frank's day would bring a group of Frank Hutmacher's friends and neighbors to his little house for a night of revelry, music, singing (the Thomases were great for initiating songfests), dancing, and card games. The card game "Whist" was popular. Frank always had an ample supply of homegrown sunflower seeds available for his guests, who would also bring food, and, of course, a gift for the honoree. It was a popular form of entertainment and camaraderie for many generations.

Me and my sideman guitar picker and lifelong friend Jack Roshau. We played many gigs together, the first one being a $5 barn dance. I still have a little squeeze box he owned. My brother Andy rescued it from a trash dumpster and gave it to me.

Back to the accordion. I sent back the buttonbox and ordered a small piano accordion for $19.95. Not too versatile but will have to do until I'm able to save enough money for a larger one. So, I learned many simple tunes, which fit the limited keyboard. At age 10, I and Jack, who played steel guitar, played our first gig, a barn dance, initiating the neighbors' new barn one mile from our house. I walked there, carrying my little accordion under my arm. Played to a happy crowd until 2 A.M. and then walked home with my little accordion under my arm and $5.00 in my pocket.

So began a turbulent, troublesome musical hobby, which would bedevil me the rest of my life. I can't decide if this talent was a gift or a curse, though the latter seems most appropriate. But I love that sound and playing that box. It puts me in another world.

It Wasn't Rock and Roll, but I Liked It

I became addicted to accordions at an early age. It was a source of great pleasure to me, but an annoyance to my parents and siblings. To them I was a pain in the butt with that thing. Almost all my time not working was spent practicing that squeeze box in this small house full of parents, brothers, and sisters. At first everyone thought it was real cute, but this soon gave way to anger, and getting shoes and other pain-inflicting objects thrown at me, especially when radios were being listened to and/or homework was in progress.

I didn't spend much time on homework, preferring to get by with a minimum-passing grade, which was 65. This also had a tendency to irritate my teachers. I sat in my desk moving my fingers with my mind on an imaginary accordion. Meanwhile Miss Wannamaker stood up front and droned on about multiplication or what the difference is between a verb and adverb.

Who needs this? I'm doing the fingering sequence for a song: *"From this valley they say you are going, I will miss your bright eyes and sweet smile, for they say you are taking my sunshine, which has brightened my way for a while."* That's what I needed to learn, or how many beavers I needed to trap, skin, and sell to Mr. Massad at the Dickinson Hide & Fur Co. to buy a larger accordion. Mr. Massad always seemed to find fault for some dumb reason to discount the furs. "The color is too light," or "You trapped it too early. It's not prime yet," he would say. He was always nagging me about something to lower the price. His daughter Martha, who worked there, was no better.

I needed privacy for practicing my expanding repertoire and to get out of that hostile, tone-deaf house. The vacant granary would do just fine during summertime. The small pile of wheat was shoveled to the far corner and covered with a tarp. I moved in my cot, a nail keg to sit on, a kerosene lantern hanging from a wire, and my beloved accordion. Life was good. At least during the months of May, June,

July, and August. I could learn lots of tunes in four months.

But my younger brother, Florian, who was a real pain in the butt to my sisters, was asked to leave the house as well. Evicted, he was. Thrown out! So a second cot was set up in the granary. He was not a fan of my accordion music either but had to tolerate it because he was homeless, and I was bigger and could beat him up (unless he got a hold of a 2x4 stick to even the odds). So, he became a compatible roommate, covering his head with a pillow, somewhat muffling the sweet strains of "Red River Valley" at 11 P.M. I was considerate of his need for sleep, moving the nail keg outside (weather permitting). Sweet music under the stars.

Playing a Few Gigs, Hunting, Trapping, and Scavenging

Since I wasn't sitting in a high school classroom following my 8th grade graduation, I had to find other means of utilizing my time. My friend Ralph Hartman and I were playing a few dance gigs, namesday parties, barn dances, birthdays, and making a few dollars. (Namesday parties were parties based on the Catholic saints' names you were given: Saint Ray, Saint Elizabeth, etc.) Mornings were devoted to livestock care, feeding, barn cleaning, hauling hay and straw, and driving siblings to school in bad weather. Afternoons were my own, so I hunted and trapped, tromping around the hills and creeks in the snow and cold in search of coyotes, rabbits, weasels, mink, badgers, and skunks—anything Dickinson Hide & Fur would give me a few dollars for.

Another fertile field for finding some cash was skinning dead animals like old horses and cattle. A horse hide could fetch up to $10 bucks. We even killed some old sick ones that were dying and then set coyote traps around the carcasses. Later, the horse's bones, when dry, were good for $20 a ton. Tail and mane hair were at a dazzling $1 per pound. So, the next time you paint your palatial residence, look at your brush and say "thanks" to old Dobbin. Or it may have been the hair of Dolly, who bucked me off into the cactus patch.

Another income source was scrap iron salvaged by dismantling nonfunctional farm machines, like the 10-foot hay rake, for example. The metal brought ten bucks a ton. Dad wasn't too keen about this.

He liked to save the bolts and nuts and had buckets full of them. "Never know when you may need one," was his rationale. Old batteries, aluminum and copper pots and pans, and kettles and leaky tubs all were in danger of being kidnapped and dumped on the scale at Dickinson Hide & Fur Co. in exchange for the almighty dollar. Capitalism at its finest! No corruption or crookedness here (unless the hide-and-fur buyer was cheating).

My oldest sister Marian found employment at Fayette. She helped out at Mrs. Little's house and minded the store. I went there often. It was where I bought my .22 caliber ammunition for my Winchester. Some years later Marian moved up to Adamski's General Store in a nearby town. At Adamski's she didn't have to test cream for butterfat content, lift ten-gallon cream cans in and out of the cooling cellar, or "candle" eggs, a process where they are held up to a light to determine if there may be a little chickie inside, thereby making an egg unsuitable for a breakfast omelet. Who wants to confront a thing like that in the morning?

The Adamskis didn't buy or trade for groceries. You went to Scheeler's on the south side of Dickinson, which did. Marian also took a liking to a farm kid who lived near the new town in which she worked, and he liked her back apparently, as the two were soon married up. I was still woefully single.

Living Life—Believe it Or Not— In a Silo

Sometimes when you are looking on the Internet, you see a story about someone who build a house in a cave or in a tree, or barn, or boat. Sounds kind of fun, huh? Well, I did that I lived in a silo (granaries or grain bin) as a teenager. Sounds rough, but it actually gave me kind a free feeling. It was pretty hard to get kicked out of that, except when the crops were harvested. It was good to be out of that house full of stone-deaf parents and siblings who had no ear for accordion music, except for Mother and Magdalen, who liked to play the old pump organ in the living room. Tillie confessed later that she would play my squeeze box when I was out in the field and she was in no danger of getting caught.

Practicing to become a virtuoso outside of the grain bin.

    Silos don't usually have windows, so it gets in hot in there in summer. So, sleeping out under the stars was a favorite option. My mattress, being a sack of corn straw, was easily dragged in and out. The hazards outside were skeeters and other night-crawling creatures that preferred crawling over instead of around snoring bodies. It was comforting to have Bob, the dog, nearby.

    Before drifting off to dreamland on a clear night, a dazzling display of billions of heavenly bodies would appear for the world to see and enjoy; twinkling, glittering meteors streaked across the sky, flaming out into little pieces like firecrackers on the 4th of July. The moon hung up there like the director of this grand symphony. Often adding to all this were the northern lights, at times shimmering from horizon to horizon, covering the entire sky. The splendor of this show was often embellished by the sound of coyotes singing out their eerie howls, perhaps serenading mates from various vantage points in the distant hills. It was a chorus of notes, unharmonic to us, but meaningful to them, I suppose.

    It is hard to sleep with this going on, so Bob would protest by barking in the direction of these noisy creatures of the wild. Dad George did not appreciate this midnight coyote concert either, stepping out of the house in his shorts. With a 30-30 carbine in hand, he fired three volleys into the air in the direction of the howling coyotes, the echoes reverberating through the hills and valleys of what seemed like the entire Dunn County. Then silence . . . Guns were also effective tools for squelching possible budding romances between humans, or uniting them. "Shotgun weddings," they were known as.

Living in granaries need not be boring. Some clear night I may again sleep out in my backyard and gaze at the heavens. But I don't have a Bob to be beside me for protection, and there's skunks back there some nights.

The Bunkhouse:
Not Exactly a 5-Star Hotel, But We Made Do

As harvest time nears, living in a grain bin becomes uncertain because the bins are needed to store the crops. But because of drought, grasshoppers, and hail, the chances of being forced out of the bin aren't too great. Nonetheless, a small yield is usually harvested in spite of nature's mean-spirited behavior. Although the nights are getting chilly, the time to move back into the anti-accordion environment house is not a pleasant thought.

So what is an alternative? The idea of a bunkhouse comes to mind. Mr. Little had one at Fayette. Here I was, 15 years old, out of school, fully educated, and destined for slavery for the next six years until I turned 21. On that very day I would load up my own car as an adult and be a free man. I would drive away from this damn farm and realize my dream of becoming a professional accordionist like Charlie Richter, Emil "Cookie" Docktor, Tom Guttenburg, Mike Dosch, and Lawrence Welk playing over WNAX Yankton, KFYR Bismarck, or KGCX Mandan. And my parents George and Barbara and their non-musical kids could sit there in their little house on the prairie crowded around the battery-operated radio hoping the battery wouldn't go dead while listening to Raymond playing a big, beautiful, rhinestone-studded 120-bass accordion in a six-piece orchestra, with saxophones, trumpets and drums and all that.

The announcer would read the long list of venues where he would be performing for the pleasure of our thousands of fans, dancing cheek to cheek to the slower sweet tunes. No more hauling manure and straw or runaway horses for me. No, sir! Everyone would be so jealous. So these were my daydreams as I sat on them hard steel seats behind teams of horses in the fields, back and forth, round and round, day after day, mowing and raking hay and plowing.

Back to the bunkhouse at Fayette: A dilapidated wood structure used to house workmen and travelers back in the wagon and stagecoach era, it was now used as a polling place for voters in the Fayette precinct and for storage. My friend Jack Roshau and I spent several nights in it while helping there during threshing time. In addition to our cots were a pile of potatoes, melons, pumpkins, and an assortment of other objects in the room.

Before retiring for the night, we were enjoying "roll your own" Bull Durham smokes. In the dim light of the lantern, we became aware of little eyes peering at us out of the semidarkness: rats' eyes. The wood floor had holes large enough to admit these rodents. They lived in the crawl space under the floor and had come up to fetch a bit of supper from the well-stocked pantry above. We threw spuds at them, blocked their exits with heavy objects they couldn't move, and went to sleep, hoping for no more invasions from below.

Getting the Kids Out of the House Part II: Building a Bunkhouse at Home

A site was selected between the house and the pig-barn-chicken-coop combo building. In the real estate market, this would be a sure winner, a home overlooking the chickens and pigs. How quaint and charming. The baby chick brooder house was close by as well. The bunkhouse would be double quaint and charming with sweet baby chicks peeping and clucking nearby.

The bunkhouse site actually was Dad's choice as was its design and size. He was thinking ahead: In six years, when his son Raymond would be gone and a famous accordionist playing over WNAX Yankton, he would have a useful utility building for doing the butchering, sausage making, and lard rendering in. This would make his wife very happy because it would keep all the rendering mess, smell, and grease out of her house. A happy wife is a good thing. She could also benefit from this choice location for her chicken butchering. There would be a flat top stove for heating tubs of water used to ease the feather-plucking part of the process. The spring with pure, clear water was a few yards away, as was a disposal facility: a bunch of hungry pigs who liked to eat chickens' innards and heads and such. Very convenient. Everything close by. A lot of steps and time saved.

Once the meat processing was out of the way, Raymond's bunkhouse would be used for hog and chicken feed storage. This would save even more time because the feed would not have to be lugged all the way from the more-distant granary, the former summer home of the accordion virtuoso. Good planning Dad!

Dad helped with the construction. (The Schmidts liked to build things.) Stones were easy to come by from crumbling homestead shacks built of stone nearby. Clay, straw, and water mixed into a sticky mud made a tough durable mortar and plaster. Windows, a door, and boards salvaged from the Bullinger house were used up, a thin concrete floor poured, and the finishing touch: wallpaper, free, courtesy of *The Killdeer Herald* newspaper. I pasted it on the walls with care. I made sure that the *Herald* correspondent Elizabeth Boehm's weekly gossip column was right side up and at eye level. Elizabeth liked to report on the dances and parties where the accordionist Raymond Schmidt and she, Elizabeth Boehm, guitarist, furnished the music. I had a little crush on Elizabeth. "Puppy love" it was known as, but she was two years older than me, so "going together" was not acceptable in those days. But we did make beautiful music together, or so it sounded to us. And besides, there was a champion speller somewhere. I couldn't get her out my mind.

The Sad Story of Philip's Birth: Burying Our Brother

Ten paces south out of the boundary fence surrounding St. Edward's Catholic Cemetery in a pasture where livestock graze, is a small concrete slab marking the grave of the infant Philip Schmidt, my brother, who was born and died unbaptized on December 22, 1942. Like all of us, according to Catholic doctrine at the time, Philip was born with the stain of "original sin," which was a direct result of our forefather Adam having eaten forbidden fruit from the Tree of Knowledge. Transmitted to all of Adam's progeny, original sin could to be cleansed only by the sacrament of baptism.

The *Catholic Encyclopedia* of 1913 was clear on the matter: In baptism the guilt of original sin is wiped out, and the soul is cleansed. As for infant baptism, it ought to be administered in the same form as in the case of adults, not in order to cleanse the children from the real original guilt, but to secure to them entrance to the Kingdom of God.

Philip, through no fault of his own, was not baptized and therefore was denied admission to the "blessed" section of the cemetery of St. Edward's. Instead he was buried in the unblessed area reserved especially for the unbaptized. Philip was then, and is today, the lone grave there. Later, the cemetery's size was reduced for easier maintenance, leaving Philip outside of its borders. Some years ago, the Killdeer Catholic parish, now the cemetery's caretaker, contacted my brother Andy about moving this grave to inside the borders. Apparently it is now acceptable for the unbaptized to be buried there. After a family conference, we decided to leave the grave as is.

Philip was born in Mrs. Frieze's house in Killdeer. She was a midwife. Dr. Smith was there as well. It must have been a difficult birth. Philip weighed 14 lbs., and Mother's life was also in peril. Dad brought Philip home early in the morning, and my sister Magdalen laid him a crib by the window. Dad then went to Uncle Florian's house and asked him to build a little casket. He also picked up my cousin Alfred to help my brother Florian and I prepare a grave.

It was a cold, gray, windy day, and the digging was hard. The topsoil was frozen, and there was heavy clay all the way down. But by mid-afternoon, we had picked and shoveled our way down to an acceptable depth. We sat down in it to get out of cold wind and waited. In due time, Dad, and the children (our younger siblings) arrived as well as Uncle Florian and Aunt Beta with baby Philip in the nice, simple, pine, homebuilt casket. Uncle Florian had painted it green, and it was still a little bit tacky.

After lowering the small casket into the grave, Aunt Perpetua led us in the Lord's Prayer (in German). We closed the grave and that was it. Everyone went home but Dad, who went to Killdeer to be with Mother. It was an emotional day for everyone, especially Dad and I assume Mother. No priest or clergyman we are aware of ever said a prayer for Philip at this remote little grave.

Doc Smith

This collection of stories would be incomplete without paying tribute to the most trusted man in the Killdeer and surrounding community, country doctor Oscar Smith M.D. His status was tall but his stature wasn't. He was a short person, just a little over 5-feet tall, and the spittin' image of Doc Adams on the popular old TV show *Gunsmoke*. His demeanor and drawl were like Doc Adams as well. He even wore a beat-up hat like Doc Adams. In other words, he was a character.

Doc Smith occupied a small wooden building on Main Street in Killdeer, where he had a reception room with several chairs, a cluttered desk, and a medicine cabinet. There was also a small restroom and the adjacent examining room. He had no receptionist or nurse. A one-man operation he was. A little bell attached to his door tinkled when opened, announcing the arrival of patients. Hearing it tinkle when he was busy stitching up an injured cowboy or whatever, he yelled, "Hello! Have a seat. I'll be out shortly."

I went to him for relief whenever I was miserable with tonsillitis. I sat in a chair as he swabbed my troublesome tonsils with three colors (red, yellow, and purple) of horrible tasting liquids till I gagged. It did kill the pain and almost me. When he finished I asked, "How much I owe you, doc?" He rubbed his chin thoughtfully.

"Got a couple bucks in your pocket?"

"Yep." I paid him.

"Thanks, Raymond. How's your folks and the kids doin' out there in them Fayette hills?" he would inquire.

"Well, Dad is having back trouble," I would say.

"You tell him to come in and see me. Maybe we can do something for it." So this is sort of how medicine was practiced in the Dirty Thirties.

Doc Smith was the first to whack the backside of just about every teeny weenie baby born within 30 miles of Killdeer for about four decades. He came there in the mid 1920s, I think. Most babies were born in the homes of the mothers or at Mrs. Frieze's, the house of a midwife who lived near Killdeer.

The Dickinson hospital was 36 miles south, a daunting distance in those days—especially in inclement weather. Besides, who would want to go there anyway? Private rooms were up to $4 a day. Who can afford that? When labor pains started kicking up, the parents of small children quickly hustled them to relatives or friend's houses to play. Doc Smith was summoned on the party-line telephone, and soon Doc's Model A Ford came speeding up the road, pedal to the metal, 40 mph top speed, leaving a cloud of dust in its wake.

Even before the dust settled, the party liners knew Barbara's or Perpetua's time had arrived, and baby shower plans were being formulated by the ladies in the community. Party lines were so wonderful. The phones rang in every home on the circuit. Listening in on other people's conversations, or "rubbering," as it was called, was a delightful bonus to be enjoyed.

When the children came home from their cousin's house, lo and behold, the "Stork" had visited and delivered a new baby sister or brother. Surprise, surprise! Today's kids are missing out on these "Stork" visits. Too bad.

Doc Smith did have several Killdeer people with good fast cars to call on when a patient needed to be transported to a hospital. There were no ambulances or small town fire departments in those days. No helicopters either.

The last time I saw Doctor Smith was in 1970 at nursing home in Dickinson. I went there to visit him and Annie Fisher, also a resident there. The lady at the front desk cautioned me. "Do not to expect too much." She had reason to warn me: Annie had reduced into a tiny diminutive human being, sitting in a chair twisting a hankie. She stared at me but had no idea who I was.

Doc was sitting in a kind of living room staring into a fireplace. I sat down next to him. He grabbed my arm and felt my pulse and then proceeded to read me the riot act. "I told you a hundred times to stop your damn drinking! That damn booze will kill you!" he thundered. "Don't be coming in here and wasting my time until you learn to behave yourself." I promised him I would try. I walked out of the nursing home depressed and wondering, "Why do these once great people's lives have to end like this?"

CROSS-COUNTRY CATTLE DRIVES

Every fall of the year around cattle-marketing time brought numerous "buyers" out to the farms and ranches. This was before livestock auctions came to be. Dad's favorite buyer was Joe Bookie. A big guy with cowboy boots and hat, Joe chewed and smoked cigars. He was a wheeler-dealer dickerer. Every year he came with a new car. The one I remember was a Hudson convertible. It was black with white sidewall tires, a white top, beautiful wooden dash panel, and leather seat, a teenager's dream.

Dad would get in the passenger seat, I in the back seat, and off we'd go out to the range, over badger holes, rocks, through brush, and across hills, and gullies to look at the cattle. Not many obstacles slowed Mr. Bookie down. He looked thoughtfully at every steer, slowly turning and chewing his cigar, lighting it, striking the match across the beautiful cherrywood dash, spitting juice in the direction of the emergency brake, and creating a stinky mess there as he pondered an offer. It was difficult thing for me, a teenaged car lover, to watch. I sure would be a big hit with the unknown speller gal in this convertible.

Mr. Bookie bought cattle from the neighbors as well, and on an appointed day, we were to deliver his beef on the hoof to the Northern Pacific stockyards in Killdeer. The annual cattle drive was comin' up. The evening before the big day, the unlucky steers and old cows were corralled, and early at first light the next morning, we started at Uncle Florian's. My cousins and I were the cowboys and on our way toward Killdeer, 18 miles ahead as the crow flies, pushing 100-plus head of beef, most of whom did not like each other.

We also had bridges to cross. The cattle didn't like those either, refusing to cross them. It just didn't feel right underfoot to them. The solution: rope one (a smaller one), drag him across the bridge, and turn him loose. Seeing one of their own on the other side gave the others confidence that it was OK to cross, so they usually followed. Calves that pooped out were caught and loaded onto the trucks following the herd. This distressed the mother cows considerably. They mooed constantly.

Farmers and cowmen along the route needed to be informed of the approaching herd, affording them time to chase their herds out of sight to avoid a regal battle of the bulls and more serious chaos. The last glitch nearing Killdeer was automobile traffic and drivers not knowing how to navigate through a herd of cattle. "Drive real slow. Weave your way through. Don't honk," they were told.

In the afternoon we arrived at the Killdeer stockyards, penned them critters up, reunited the calves with their bellowing, frightened moms, unsaddled our frustrated sweaty horses, watered them, and rewarded them with a little pile of oats. Mr. Bookie was on hand to thank us for a job well done and hauled us to Saby's bar for lunch and R & R (rest and relaxation).

Burgers and Beer Following the Cattle Drive

Saby's was a popular Cowboy watering hole owned and operated by Mrs. Saby, a widow. At the end of the bar was an iron grill and a cigarette-smoking cook frying us four and other cow punchers big thick juicy burgers with slices of onion and lots of store-bought catsup (which was better than the homemade stuff). Beer was on tap. Nobody "carded" or checked IDs. Who cares, a buck is a buck. There may not even have been a law against underage drinking then.

We sat at the bar, boots on the brass rail, among farmers, ranchers, and carpenters all scarfing down burgers and beer. The pool tables in the backroom provided entertainment for the next two hours before Mr. Bookie came by and hauled us back to the stockyards and our horses in his cigar-spit-stinky Hudson convertible. What a shame. Pitiful, that was to behold. I don't remember him paying us anything other than buying the beer and burgers.

We saddled up and started for home. The sun was setting, and we went riding along. We had to kick the ponies to a gallop when passing a stockwater pond to keep from being chewed up by skeeters. I got home at 11 P.M., just in time to listen to the Three Suns on the radio. The Suns were a trio from New York and featured an accordionist—a good one. I listened every night.

Manning, a village nine miles east of us, was the place to be seen on Friday nights. The Manning Community Club, a local ladies charity organization, put on dances as fundraisers, charging 75-cents admission. Seventy percent of the proceeds went to the bands. Sam and his City Fellers was my favorite. Sam played clarinet like nobody else could.

We danced from 9 AM to 1:30 PM, with an intermission, at which time you could buy and eat lunch with the girl you may have asked earlier to dine with when dancing with her. Or, you could go to Ray Walker's bar down the street and enjoy your favorite hooch, providing you could get near it through the crowd.

Differences of opinion between guys were often settled with fighting. This sometimes resulted in combatants spending time looking out through the bars of the jail across the street, as I and others did one night for trying to help my Uncle Carl . He was getting beat up by a big guy, and the sheriff threw us all in the slammer till the end of the dance. So, we missed out on the lilting strains of "Home Sweet Home" emanating from Sam's clarinet, and someone else danced cheek to cheek with the girl with whom I ate lunch earlier. Damn, damn, damn! We were released after the dance ended, and everyone went on their way home.

BLOODHOUNDS IN THE FIELDS

Often we hear the term "dumb animals" used. This may be a misnomer. Some of their activities are amazing. One day I was working a field. A small herd of antelope were grazing in an adjacent pasture. Five animals resembling greyhounds appeared on a nearby knoll, huddling, as in a conference, eyeing the antelope and formulating a plan for catching a tasty lunch.

I shut down the tractor and watched this scenario unfold. The Kaspers, a couple who ranched five miles to the southwest were reputed to be raising "bloodhounds," and they had been seen roaming the area. I assumed these five characters to be of this ranch. The plan: Each hound positioned itself as if it were a point on a five-point star. They did so very carefully so as not to spook the prey. At a signal of some sort, they started running in a circle, allowing all but one of the startled deer to escape. An orchestrated ritual ensued, five hounds taking turns chasing this unfortunate helpless antelope in a circular pattern round and round until it was exhausted.

A half-hour later, five contented hounds were lying on the grass and taking themselves a leisurely nap, after having enjoyed their feast. Life was good. Nearby were the bones and remnants of their dinner, which were now being fought over by a few hungry magpies. So I cranked up the McCormick and resumed my farming, thinking that animals must able to talk to each other without actually saying anything. Amazing, isn't it?

Want Some Ice?
You Will Have to Go and Cut It Out of the River!

Back in the days when there no refrigerators, lowering foods in boxes and pails into cool wells and stock water tanks was a routine chore. It extended the life of perishables somewhat but was makeshift at best. Iceboxes were the preferred option. We managed to afford one of these wonders in the early 1940s. Quite a handsome piece of furniture it was; hardwood oak, about the size of a refrigerator. It had three compartments: the top one for ice blocks, the center being the largest for food items, and the lower for the buckets catching water from the melting ice. Some creative folks with ice boxes installed drains through the wall out to the gardens.

The ice house required us to do a deep excavation into the side hill between the house and spring. Posts, tree branches, straw, and dirt formed the roof, and a small access door completed the project. Harvesting ice is only possible following a hard cold winter, which is usually not a problem in N.D. We did so from the middle of the stock pond or the mighty Knife River. A special ice saw was used to cut blocks about a foot wide and deep. A long plank was lowered under the floating ice blocks and pulled up onto the surface with the help of ice hooks and loaded on a sled. We hauled home the blocks and stacked them tightly into the ice house, which was insulated on all sides, top and bottom, with straw and a tarp (this was before sheeting plastic was invented). As ice was needed, someone would lift the door aside, crawl in the house, clip ice tongs around a block, and lift it out.

Homemade ice cream was the greatest benefit of having an ice supply. It was a Sunday treat usually. Kids would fight about who got to sit on the freezer to stabilize it as it was being cranked. Then there was the battle about who got to lick the paddles after they were removed from the container, this reward usually going to the hard worker who did the cranking. No easy task!

For those readers not familiar with ice cream freezers, they are a device about the size of a five-gallon bucket with a smaller one-gallon stainless steel container within. This leaves space all around for crushed ice. A geared apparatus with a handle for cranking activates paddles, which go round and round. You understand?

The ingredients were real cow cream, eggs, vanilla, and sugar. Artery clogging at its best, but mmmmm goood. . . .

Mining Coal to Heat Your Own House

Winters were unpredictable in North Dakota, Some were mild, but most were cold and miserable, so it was necessary to prepare for miserable. The popular option was mining your own coal. There were several nearby mines that sold coal. They were owned by farmers with coal seams on their land, which they developed and mined and loaded for the customers for $3 a ton. City folks were their market.

These little coal mines were underground seams of coal of various thicknesses ranging from 3 ft. to 8 ft. The average was about 4 ft. The "overburden," or amount of soil atop the seam, was anywhere from between 4 and 10 feet thick and consisted of compacted clay. It was tough stuff to strip off, requiring plowing and in some cases, explosives, dynamite, or blasting powder to jar it loose. It was removed with a horse-drawn, shovel-like device called a fresno, which had a handle on it to control the filling. The handle could flip the operator off and into the air if the leading edge snagged an object such as a stone. Broken ribs resulted at times.

Dad's favorite mine was one mile east on Mr. Hutmacher's land. We had a threshing machine and threshed his grain in exchange for coal. It took about six days of plowing and scraping to remove the overburden. We packed a lunch for ourselves and grain for the horse team. At lunchtime we would sit in this pit, eat, and rest, and enjoy a smoke or two, picking apart chunks of clay with fissures containing the remains of weird insects and imprints of leaves. Geologists would have liked this. This archeological stuff must be still down there, buried forever.

Another entertainment feature of the lunch hour was watching garter snakes charming or hypnotizing frogs. Ponds of stagnant green water abounded with stones protruding, snakes and frogs sunning themselves on them. Mr. Snake would slither to within 12 inches or so of his prey, lay real still, and stare. Kermit the frog was transfixed by this invisible magnetic force and inched forward very, very slowly. Bad move. In a split second Mr. Snake struck, and the frog became a bulge in its belly.

Time to get back to mining coal: It needs to be blown up. Holes were drilled into the coal by twisting on a hand-operated drill to a depth of three feet. A couple of handfuls of blasting powder were poured down a hole, the fuse lowered to it, and another handful of powder was followed by a rag or wad of paper. Clay was tamped down on top with a crowbar till it was full. Then we would light the fuse, run for the wagon, and get the horses out of there because they didn't like the KABOOM and coal flying high.

Next we had to heave the resulting sooty hunks of BTUs on the wagon and haul them home and into the coal bin in the basement of our house. We "mined" two loads a day for a week. Oh yes, the basement. We added it years after the house was built. We dug it by hand a shovelful at a time, finishing the job by building stone walls around the perimeter. A furnace was also installed. We were getting kind of "modern."

Butchering Pigs

This is not for the faint-hearted. "Gross," some of you will find it to be. After harvesting and coal mining were tended to, around mid-October, when the flies and other pests had retired for the season and the days were sort of cold, it was time to put up the winter's meat supply. The Schmidts had bunch of kids who walked to and from school and fetched and milked cows and fed pigs and chickens and cleaned barns and did a bunch of other stuff every day. These kids burned up lots of energy and needed lots of meat, pork, beef, and poultry to eat.

Butchering day required many hands, so it was a community event. Uncle Florian and Aunt Perpetua (yep, that was her name) came by on the appointed day. A scalding tank, usually a 55-gallon steel barrel with the end removed, was used. It was tilted at a 45-degree angle, filled about half full with water, propped up somehow, a fire blazing underneath. A low bench-like "scraping table" was placed at the open end. The porkers (ham-and-bacon and sausages to be) were penned nearby. A rifleman with a .22 (usually me; we skipped school on butchering days) and a blood catcher with a kettle stood by as did a guy with a sharp knife. I think I'll skip the next action. . . . Oh hell, you may as well know how morbid this was. It was old stuff to us. A rifle shot stunned and dropped the pig. The butcherer stabbed it between the front legs, aiming for the heart to get a good blood flow going, which was captured by the kettle holder, usually my mother or auntie. It was necessary to keep stirring this stuff to keep it from clotting, so she would plop the kettle into nearby snow bank and stir it until it was cold. This was added to "blood sausage," a delicacy popular at the time.

Next, the dead porker was dragged to the scalding vat, submerged in the scalding tank head first, and spun around several times until its hair let go. He was then pulled out and reversed to scald his rear half as well, after which he was pulled out onto the table. Everyone then pitched in to scrape off all of the hair. Then the carcass was hung by the rear feet on a nearby scaffold, the belly slit open, and gutted carefully. Two people holding a large tub caught the innards, which were carried to the kitchen for the crew there to separate the various organs: liver, lungs, heart, stomach, small and large intestines, etc., to be prepared and cleaned.

So while this crew was busy getting started doing their thing, the next pig is getting . . . you know. Sometimes as many as six a day sacrificed their lives. Cleaning "casings" for sausage making is somewhat distasteful. Better not go into detail here. Are you still reading?

Processing Pork

So now the pork is on the hook and daylight is fading. The next phase, cutting it up, is done in the house. There is no electricity, so lamps hang from the ceiling. Pork halves are plopped on one end of the table and are cut into hams, shoulders, bacon, and spare ribs. The trimmings go into a tub to be ground up for sausage. A hand crank grinder was clamped on the table edge with a perspiring, protesting kid cranking away (brother Florian). Hard work. Had to rotate crankers often (sister Magdalen). Mother and Perpetua are busy cleaning up the pig heads for cooking as they will become blood sausage and head cheese. The feet are also prepared for pickled pigs' feet. There is also a tub for excess fat, which will become lard (shortening) as well as laundry soap. These tasks are done at a later time. Next week.

The tub of ground trimmings is now seasoned with spices. There is usually a somewhat heated discussion about whose favorite recipe to use and how much garlic and paprika, etc., should go in. Sausage making was a big deal in the community. Everyone thought theirs was the tastiest recipe. The sausage-making machine was a device with a hopper and crank and spigot for slipping casings onto. By now, the casings, which have been washed many times and inverted and soaked in saltwater are filled and cut into about two-foot lengths with a twist in the middle for easier hanging in the smokehouse. The sausage smoking will be done tomorrow.

My mamma with her four youngest kids at the time: Magdalen, me, Florian, and Marian (from left to right). We were too young here to do any butchering but one day would.

It is nearing midnight, and Uncle Florian and Auntie Perpetua head for home, wondering what their kids have been up to that day. They take with them unsmoked sausage for the next morning's breakfast. On another day, George and Barbara will go to Uncle's place, and this butchering day will repeat itself there but on a larger scale because they have more kids: older ones, Paul and Tony. This helps.

The sausages are smoked about three hours. Hardwood smoke is preferred. Broken tool handles were saved and burned for this purpose. The other pork was packed into wooden barrels, covered with a brine of water, vinegar, salt, spices, and tenderizer. Next spring it would also be smoked for about three days.

Head cheese utilizes the tongues and odds-and-ends of skin, ears, and noses of pigs. It is precooked and seasoned and packed into the scrubbed and scraped, inverted pig stomachs. Then it is cooked some more. Yummy! Lard rendering (cooking fat) yielded shortening and "cracklings" for making laundry soap. So much for butchering pigs. Fun, huh?

Mrs. Little, the Telephone Man, and Me

Mrs. Isabelle Little and her husband Frank established Fayette. Mr. Little sold land and farm machinery, leaving her to run the store. She was a kind, generous, caring lady, During the Depression she made sure that those who needed help got it. She charged groceries to families, and many never did pay their bills. When we acquired Fayette, I found a ledger on a shelf in the store. The ledger documented these unpaid accounts.

Mrs. Little had a Model T Ford "coupe" as two-seaters were called. It was one of the later ones, a 1927 maybe. But she wasn't the best driver and didn't like to drive. The story goes she didn't stop in time once and went through a fence and down a ravine in front of her stone house. A grove of wild June berries brought the T to a soft stop. She wasn't hurt and got out, but the Ford caught fire and burned up. She was carless for some time until a wealthy friend or relative from Maine presented her with a new, black, "streamlined" 1934 Ford V8, four-door sedan.

A beautiful car it was. It had a smooth, powerful engine and a nice soft ride that was totally befitting for a lady like Isabelle Little. But she was afraid to drive it after several disastrous attempts, so Annie Fisher usually drove. However, Annie was busy at the store, so she would call me to chauffeur Mrs. Little around to check the area's rickety telephone system when it went on the fritz, which was often.

This system consisted of utilizing the wires of farmers' fences. As long as there were no breaks or disconnect between farms and no rain to short it out, it worked quite well. But there were ongoing maintenance problems. One day Mrs. Little called Art, the Bell Telephone repairman from Dickinson, and told him to come to our house, pick me up, and teach me how to maintain the phone system.

Art and I rode the lines in his utility pickup. He taught me to climb poles. "Always remember to keep your butt and belly away from the pole so the spurs sink in," he cautioned. Splice wires, replace insulators, and reset rotted-off poles. I knew how to do this already, so this was easy. He left me with a set of climbing spurs, a tool kit, and extra insulators. "Damn kids with .22s shoot them off," he grumbled about the insulators. (But he didn't leave me a telephone man's pickup, the cheapskate.) So, I was the Fayette Central Telephone Co. repairman for a short time, until it was rebuilt with tall poles and smooth wire, the livestock fences having been abandoned. I never got paid for fixing these phone lines. It was a community service I performed, I guess.

Meanwhile, I was often behind the wheel of the Ford V8, with Mrs. Little beside me with a "car robe" tucked around her legs in cold weather because the heaters in cars were not very efficient. Often they didn't work at all. She talked constantly, commenting on the beauty of the landscape and crops. Good thing she didn't drive. She never looked at the road.

My First Band

The Fayette community was filled with music and lots of musical talent. I grew up believing that music was part of the normal person's mind. Musical instruments were in all homes. Guitars, fiddles, banjos, and accordions lay around like pillows on couches. Pump organs were a standard living room fixture, a custom brought over from the old country, perhaps. Today it is the TV and computer.

Social gatherings often evolved into songfests after someone picked up and began strumming a guitar. The Thomas family members were all good musicians, Mr. Thomas having been a teacher and choral conductor in Germany. They had eight children and were the nucleus of the St. Edward's church choir. Others were the

Hartmans and the Schmalzes. This was a world-class group, second to none other out there on the North Dakota prairie. Saturday- and Sunday-night socializing often consisted of a community dance in the Hartman's hayloft or vacant granaries. People brought instruments, played dance music, and sang and drank home-brewed beer, which was available free for the taking from bottles cooling in the stock water tank nearby. Nobody got intoxicated or unruly. It was just a sociable community of nice folks singing and dancing and having a good time.

From these pickin's and squeezin's the Melody Kings were born. I was the accordionist. This group became quite popular, playing gigs around the area and making some money. I had bought a larger accordion and learned more tunes and fancy arpeggios in my quest to move ever closer to my WNAX dream.

The Kings' closest competitors were the Knife River Ramblers, a pretty good quartet of young Russians. Unlike the Kings, the Ramblers had a drummer and saxophone. They were a great-sounding group—a real threat. We competed, each band carving out its own niche. Later we would become good friends with these guys.

The nagging issue in all this was transportation to the gigs. My dad hated this activity of mine and was reluctant about me using his car or truck for this "nonsense." I needed a car of my own. That's all there was to it! Johnny W. had a '31 Chevie coupe that I would die for, and he had it for sale. He had married Anna H., with whom he had eloped one night because Anna's folks didn't like him as he was Hungarian. Now he needed a bigger car because Anna is, you know.

My First Car: A '31 Chevy

I looked over at Johnny's Chevy after Sunday Mass at St. Edward's parking lot. Beautiful! Maroon body. Black fenders. Chrome headlights and radiator. The car had a fold-up luggage carrier in addition to the spacious trunk, with lots of space for the professional-sized accordion. I would soon have two spare wheels and tires, one in each front fender, with chrome covers. Brown upholstery. A teenaged guy's dream. What girl wouldn't want to be seen riding with me in this car? Sinful thoughts . . . Oh, my gosh! Just after communion yet. That spelling champion, whoever or wherever she was, would be impressed for sure.

Johnny W. was asking $125. I had about $50. Where to get the other $75? Not from Dad. I was sure of that. My sister Marian had been working for Mrs. Little at Fayette. I would beg on my knees if need be and repay her back with interest within a year, I promised. I would take her along to dances—anything. She succumbed to my wailing and whining and I walked to Johnny W's house three miles distant and drove home with mine and Marian's Chevrolet Coupe. A dream come true. But something was puzzling. I wasn't playing any dances. Had the Melody Kings been wiped out by those Ramblers? The Ramblers were good. Having a drummer gave them a nice beat that dancers liked. The Kings lacked somewhat a good solid beat.

After one Sunday Mass, my fellow band members kind of shunned me. Something fishy was going on here. I later heard that I had been replaced by Lena, Ralph and Pauline's older sister. Lea, as she preferred to be called (she hated "Lena" because it was too Russian sounding), played well and was a great dancer. I always thought she liked to dance more than play a squeeze box. I speculated that her parents decided three kids making music money was better than two. Sacked I was—overthrown by my own band! Kicked out. Exiled. Friendships ruined, all for a few dollars. And here I have a '31 Chevy to pay for.

I formed a new trio with some other musicians and played a few gigs, but it didn't go well, so we disbanded. My parents were happy. "Musicians lead the parade to hell," my grandpa often chided me. It was time to give some serious thought to farming. Yeah, sure. It's been raining some, so things are looking good for farming. I drove to Dickinson one Saturday afternoon to get a haircut and then to the Hiway Inn to dance with some girls and listen to Harry Cooke's Orchestra. P.S. Lea: I really wasn't mad at you. How could I be? You were so lovely...

Joining a New Band

Harry Cooke was a barber in his early forties. He had a belly that reminded me of the cartoon character Mr. Dithers, Dagwood Bumstead's boss. Harry also had a popular five-piece band but no accordionist. I asked him why. "There aren't any good ones around.

Lots of bad ones and none play popular music, only three-chord waltzes and polkas, and no one can read the music," he said. I told him I did (read music) but not real well and was learning.

Harry said he and his band would be playing a gig on Friday. He told me to bring my accordion, "sit in" with his band, and see how it goes. I did, and I stayed and played the whole gig with all the Melody Kings members at the dance looking up at me from the floor. Oh sweet, sweet revenge it was!

I played accordion with the Harry Cooke band for five years. Then the Cookes moved to Pasadena, Calif. We were a busy group, playing three events a week. There were many more in June. Lots of wedding dances and wedding marches on church steps as the happy couples came by. The band was in demand for high school proms because we played the newest popular songs. Harry's daughter, the pianist, had a great voice and sang. The kids liked that.

Another niche we filled was anniversaries. I remember John and Hattie B's 50th. They claimed there was not a single angry word exchanged in the 50 years, and they had sex every night. Often twice! Hard to beat a life like that. I enjoyed being a part of this good popular band, and the WNAX dream faded into the background. By now I had a 1940 Plymouth sedan. Life was good.

Back on the farm my parents fumed, worrying about my nights out but more about my moral behavior. Musicians had reputations—wine, women, and song, the legend went. "He'll get killed out there some night, and what about girls?" they fretted. "Have all the confessions and communions gone for nothing? He hasn't been to St. Edward's since he started with this Cook guy, or whatever his name is." (I stayed in Dickinson overnight and went to St Joseph's.) "He'll be bringing home a knocked-up girl—wait and see."

They needn't have worried. I behaved myself. Mother's teaching had soaked in. I always made sure that my farming duties were attended to. It was sometimes hard, being dog tired, but I got 'er done.

Life Before Plumbing and Electricity

One of the more annoying inconveniences of rural life up north was too much darkness. The ample daylight of summer (5 AM to 8 PM) was great and well utilized. But the winter nights were agonizingly long. Before electricity lit up the country's homes, an assortment of devices was utilized to counter this blackness. Kerosene lamps with wicks and glass chimneys were most popular, if not the safest alternative. They sat in the center of tables and night stands, flickering anemic circles of light. Boxes of matches you could strike on any surface were usually nearby as well. Meanwhile, bunches of energetic, active kids were usually running and climbing here and there and zipping around the room. Mother's watchful eyes were on these rambunctious offspring: "Rayman, and Maggalen, you get away from der, and behave yoself. You gonna knock the light over and burn the house down . . . then what we gonna do?" she would yell.

For the barns there were lanterns with handles for carrying and hooks for hanging on pegs in the walls. A hazardous environment it was, with combustible hay and straw scattered about everywhere. It was easy to picture the cow kicking over the lantern and burning down the entire farmstead.

My brother Florian and I lived and bunked upstairs in the attic of our house. We hung lanterns on nails driven into the rafters. Then there was a "fancy" lamp in the living room for use when company came. It sat on our ornate wooden end table, the one with the statue of the Blessed Virgin Mary on it. We prayed the rosary before it on the hardwood floor when the weather and the road were too bad to go to St. Edwards on Sunday. Oh, this was so agonizing. Kneeling there through 55 Hail Marys plus other petitions, like praying for those souls in Purgatory.

Whenever we did an overnight stay at our Uncle Jacob and Aunt Rose's house in Dickinson, electric light bulbs hung from the ceiling. They were lit with the pull of a nice golden chain with a little glass ball on the end of it. Pure luxury, it was. Also Auntie had an electric motor on her Maytag washer. Nice and quiet, only the gentle sound of the water sloshing around in there.

My mother's Maytag washer was not electric. It was fueled by a noisy, stinky, gas-oil mix engine with a long flex hose sticking outside through a hole in the wall. It was a perfect place for mice and snakes to sneak in. Like most houses, it sat in our utility room, which was a small space where everyone entered the house to wash up and shed their coats and galoshes after completing their daily duties or, if you were a kid, playing in the dirt pile with the dogs and pet frogs. There was a wash basin but no running water. Instead there was a bar of soap on a cabinet, a bucket of water, and a "dipper," which was sorta like a soup ladle. The wash basin, which wasn't plumbed, had to be emptied into a slop pail sitting nearby. Kitchen waste went into another bucket to feed the pigs who squealed in anticipation when they saw it coming and then fought each other to get at it. (I would watch these greedy hogs and the thought came to me that I would almost certainly be eating them after butchering day.)

Washing up was usually with room-temperature water. If hot was desired, a teakettle was available from the wood/coal/cow chip/fired stove around the corner, in the adjacent kitchen. A barrage of orders and suggestions came from the mother of the house: "You see to it that you refill that pail," she would shout. "Don't you set foot in here with those dirty overshoes and look at the dog hair on ya! Git outside and brush 'em off!"

Shall we talk about the disgusting topic of bathrooms? Might as well. New homes built by immigrants in North Dakota were often constructed of native sandstone bonded together with gumbo, a form of clay dug out of the ground. The walls were often two-feet thick to counter the high winds on the prairie and retain warmth inside. This was very effective. The houses were also cool inside in the summertime. In appearance, they looked like adobe homes in Arizona and New Mexico.

But, of course, these homes and others for many years had no plumbing, no bathrooms, and nowhere to go potty. Plumbing wouldn't come until much later. Even when it did, "going inside" was sort of unthinkable. What kind of slobby person would stink up the house? It was disgusting to even think of it. Please. Do it behind the barn or bushes.

Later, outhouses came into use. To build one, you would dig a pit in an obscure site, maybe behind the car shed. About four-feet deep should do (depending on how many kids you've got). In North Dakota, it was best to face the outhouse southeast and downwind so the door didn't flap around on windy days when the breeze was blowing in from the north. Add a Montgomery Ward catalog and you were all set—in sync with the times.

But people still kept white-enamel "pots" in their bedrooms during the cold winter nights and emptied them the next day so they didn't have to venture out to the outhouse. The boys' sleeping quarters with windows that opened kind of eliminated the need for potties. "What the heck are them yellow blotches in the snow?" my mother would yell. "Don't tell me you didn't do that!"

Later on with septic tanks it became practical and possible to live like our city cousins with plumbing. But you might be surprised to know that many older folks were still reluctant to embrace the indoor "throne." They thought it was gross. I didn't feel that way. It sure beat making that midnight outhouse trip through the snow. And them catalog pages. Geez! Glad to get rid of them.

Powering Up: Homemade Electricity

In them so called good old days, the mid-1940s and thereabouts, rural North Dakotans were thinking of getting modernized. They wanted to be in step with the rest of the country and have the luxury of electricity like their city cousins who started and stopped everything with the touch of a button or the flip of a switch.

Here we were in the country sitting out there on the prairies and steppes, living a primitive, behind-the-times lifestyle. Milking cows, pumping water, cranking the cream separator twice a day by hand—pure drudgery. Also there was the corn sheller, a seed cleaning machine we had to crank round and round by hand. Tiresome. Boring. Mother threatened us kids with beatings if we complained. In the shop there were hand-operated tools, saws, drills, grinders. These were hard chores. If only there was electricity to make life easier.

Frank and Isabel Little's house and their store at Fayette had a "Delco light plant," it was called. It was a noisy, gasoline-powered engine that drove a generator and ran constantly. It was installed in a remote shed to minimize noise. The store and their house were nice and bright with electric lights.

My Uncle Florian thought these "light plants" were man's greatest invention ever, so he bought one and installed it in his farmhouse. He must have decided putting up with the racket of an engine running constantly was not too high a price for enjoying bright lights. My parents visited there, wondering how the heck he could afford this extravagant luxury. It was a 110-volt system city-folks used. It required 52 costly two-volt batteries to run it. But it was nice sitting there at his dining room table while playing cards with a bright electric light shining down over them. Still there was this darned constant annoying engine noise.

Then came Roy Dowel. Roy was from Detroit City, Mich. He was what we called a "high tuner" electrician. We looked up to him because he was so smart about electricity, a rarity in our rural community. Roy had an idea: Create, build, sell, and install wind-powered, 32-volt electrical systems. If he was going to stay in the area and support his new wife Ellen and himself, and possibly kids, he needed an income.

Somewhere in a big eastern city, maybe Minneapolis, wind-powered 32-volt electrical systems were being manufactured by the Wincharger Co. The Wincharger system was a neat outfit, but far too costly for most farmers who were still reeling from the hard times of the Great Depression. Also appearing on shelves of hardware stores were 32-volt motors for power tools, like grinders, saws, drills, and motors. If we had 32-volt electricity, we could use those tools. Very tempting.

Roy gathered up discarded large electric motors and rewired them, converting them to 32-volt generators. He knew how to do this. A nearby young German farmer named Frank Shiller partnered up with Roy. Frank was an expert mechanic. He modified his tractor's engines to increase its power and speed instead of buying a larger one. Frank was also a woodcraftsman. Together, he and Roy's mission was to electrify these North Dakota farmers.

Frank made the propellers for the electrical systems by whittling them out of hardwood. The three-bladed propellers he crafted were aerodynamically perfect. They were similar in design but smaller than those we see scattered over the nation's landscape nowadays. These props were mated up with Roy's generators and the units mounted on top of 30-foot high windmill towers in the farmyards. Wiring was brought from the generator down to a bank of sixteen 2-volt batteries all connected to one another. They formed a sturdy 32 volt-system that provided stored power when the wind didn't blow. Roy also wired in outlets and lights in the houses, shops, and barns of his customers.

My dad bought one of these systems. Setting it up on the tall tower and watching the glistening blades spin filling the batteries with invisible power was an exciting event. Like pure magic. The neighbors would be jealous. Dad bought motors, one for mom's

Maytag. She was the happiest person in the county. We had an electric grindstone for sharpening tools, an electric drill, and then electrified the dreaded hard-to-turn cream separator and, of course, lights shown everywhere. House. Shop. Barn. A light mounted on a tall pole in the middle of the yard lit up the outside like the one at the Fayette Mercantile. When company came and went home later in the dark it was turned on until they were safely in their automobiles. A nice touch of graciousness. These faithful, trouble-free, workhorse power plants served many area farmers for many years.

Roy Dowel and Frank Shiller's 2-volt-electricity generating shop went out of business as the Rural Electrical Administration (REA) made its way across the countryside. The REA was a federal agency whose goal was to provide more efficient higher voltage power to the country—and clutter the once-pristine countryside with poles, towers, and cables. Progress, it was called.

Nonetheless, the high-voltage electricity provided by the REA made farm folks happy. Unlike the 32-volt systems, they always had unlimited electric power at their fingertips. The REA also was a boon to city businesspeople, especially the hardware-store owners. Farmers with this newly acquired 110-volt power were hungry for new electric tools; drills, saws, grinders, water tank heaters and other tools. Country women no longer heated their irons with hot coal or wood fired ranges to straighten clothes. Our battery operated radios went into the storage sheds. We didn't throw them away because they still worked. But now the power never died during the middle of Gene Autury singing *Back in the Saddle Again* or Lawrence Welk playing the *Beer Barrel Polka*.

Love Letters: Desperately Seeking Marie

My mother subscribed to a weekly newspaper printed in German called the *North Dakota Herald*. It catered to the many German settlers in the area who, unlike my mother, could not read English. She read both. She often tried to teach me to read German, but I saw no need for that. After all, this was the USA. I wish I had listened to her because it would have been good to know during World War II.

The *Herald* featured a "Young Folks Page" in English. The page provided teenagers a forum to express their views on anything and/or everything, whatever topic might create a barrage of responses for or opposed to it. The big subjects being the moral issues facing young adults: heavy-weight issues like is cheek-to-cheek dancing OK if you're not going steady or engaged? What's the limit on a skirt length before it borders on sinful? Should a girl ask a guy to dance? All important stuff. I was a contributor as you may guess, putting my 2-cents worth in on various issues. I asked a question, "Does anyone reading this page know a girl named Marie Commes?" I told of the spelling contest, often wondered where or who she was, and whether she would like to exchange letters or be pen pals. She could write to me at Raymond Schmidt, Manning, N.D. This was the best I could do at the time. There was no Facebook or Twitter back then.

Well it so happened that Henry and Mary Commes, Marie's grandparents, were subscribers and read the *Herald*, so they read and forwarded my appeal to their granddaughter Marie. Soon thereafter, Mr. Liess, our wonderful mailman, delivered a letter addressed in graceful handwriting, to Raymond Schmidt, Manning, N.D. In the upper left-hand corner: From Marie E. Commes, Box 63, Halliday, N.D. I was excited and scared. What am I getting myself into here? Suppose she's the banker's daughter at Halliday or not Catholic? What if she's got a boyfriend and is engaged? Maybe I should have maybe left well enough alone. The handwriting was just too, too perfect. And here I am living in a bunkhouse next to the hog and chicken barn.

"Dear Mr. Schmidt," the letter started. "Allow me to take the liberty to fulfill your request made in the paper. Your letter was sent to me by my sister. It was indeed a pleasant surprise. The only fly in the ointment is I don't remember you as well as you deserve to be after taking the trouble to get in touch with me. Are you conducting a campaign for pen pals or a survey to find out how many level-headed straight shootin' girls are out there? Clear up the matter, please."

Thus began a flow of letters building a romance and marriage, which would endure for nearly 70 years and counting. It's a lifelong "getting to know each other" relationship that continues to this day.

Another Letter to Marie

"Dear Marie: The last day of the wild little month of February brought your very welcome letter. I knew it was coming that very day as I had a dream the night before. When something special is about to happen, I often get a preview of its impending arrival. Perhaps this was only a coincidence. Your letter's arrival signaled that the road was passable, so I did some driving for my parents' interests. Dad's pavement-hugging Olds was no match for the snow depth, so my Chevy was called into action. One trip took me to Killdeer. I saw Reverend Spegele's new Studebaker parked downtown, almost demolished. This man drives like an insane wild man. 'St. Christopher is with me,' he says. The Reverend had Mass at St. Ed's Sunday, but no one came.

I also made a trip to Dickinson, where I bought a few sheets of music and checked out a book, the "Theory of Flight," to break the monotony of long winter nights. The kids at Prospect #1 don't like the teacher, Miss Boe. Seems she is not real interested in her duties or pupils that her vocation demands. In her opinion, not all children are born equal, so she came uncomfortably close to being terminated. Have you reached a decision on enlisting in the Women's Army Auxiliary Corp. (WAAC)? I understand there is now also an organization consisting of women Marines. Will there be a time when there are no wars? Getting back to your letter, I'm sorry I misunderstood about you being in the convent. This came from a second cousin of mine, who apparently knew you and thought you were. I have a cousin, Sr. Macaria, a Benedictine. Her brother Charles Schmidt has a bar in Richardton. A nun and a bartender. Some combination.

You should hear Reverend Spegele preach on the subject of 'Higher State of Life' about priesthood and sisterhood. He keeps looking at me. The Rev. S. has organized the youth of the parishes into a St. Francis Xavier Society, he calls it. Its purpose is to raise money for church needs by producing stage plays in area theaters and small town halls. They are fun to do, but time consuming. It also teaches acting skills. This summer you may enjoy 'Aaron Slick from Punkin' Crick' and 'Hobgoblin House' in the Halliday city hall.

I must end this letter as brother Florian is in the room with me with a saxophone he borrowed from somewhere, and the notes coming from this musician-never-to-be are not conducive to the thought process. Please write soon. Could you send a picture of yourself? I know you are very beautiful. Sincerely, Raymond."

Another Letter from Marie

"Dear Raymond. You are a mighty lucky fellow having all your premonitions coming true! Mine seldom do, but then maybe I have all too many. No I don't think dreams are always superstitious. Experts on the topic say we dream at night of the things we thought of during the day. This being true, then commonsense figures will almost tell us what 'might' happen tomorrow. You know two and two are four. Or is it five? This explanation may satisfy some people, but it doesn't account for those ridiculously foolish and funny things we visualize in our dreams. Absolutely unthought of, less yet unheard of. For instance, being endowed with a pair of gold trimmed, diamond studded gossamer wings and performing magic stunts of all kinds. It's a good thing I'm not in the habit of dreaming daily, unless it were day dreaming.

Here's hoping the roads are again in normal condition. Our period of isolation lasted almost nine weeks. One evening we enjoyed an excellent turkey supper at the neighbor's, the occasion being the birthday of one of their sons. Saturday evening we saw the movie of Gene Autrey, *Down Wyoming Way*. Enjoyed it immensely. Did you chance to see it? *Gone with the Wind* is showing in Dickinson this weekend. I saw that two summers ago. The coloring was magnificent, but the plot in itself is not what expectations had it.

It is surprising to know that Lyla is your cousin. We were classmates for three years. She graduated a year before I did. I chanced to meet her in Dickinson during Thanksgiving vacation. I was embarrassed when I asked her what she was doing and was told she was married and a 'housekeeper.' I resent the word. Homemaker would be much more befitting. Do you agree? It is out of our good homes that become ardent, faithful, and zealous citizens. We teachers notice that, particularly in our pupils. It is the poorly managed homes that present us with discipline cases. No 'housekeeper' would take care of all these little perplexing problems, but a 'homemaker' would.

Vocational problems can be very perturbing. These priests usually have a foresight into the lives of those they recommend or suggest for any particular state of life. Most often they are absolutely correct. From a seed can grow a mighty sturdy plant. In this case a seed could be in the form of a small thought, even neglected it can gnaw on one's conscience and gradually become a reality. Does this sound like advice? Gee, I hope not. Grandpa always said I was cut out to be a politician or a lawyer."

Dear Marie

"Dear Marie: Thank you for your exemplar letter. I was favorably impressed and enjoyed reading it. I'd suggest you give some thought to journalism, sharing your thoughts and wisdom with the world's people. I'm wondering if I should answer a letter such as you write, they are so skillfully composed. The nuns at Richardton must have been excellent teachers. I never got to go to high school, so had to do my best to educate myself as best I could utilizing the 'school of hard knocks,' as they say. Would have answered your letter sooner, but was in Dickinson painting Grandma's house—no small task for one person. I'm not done yet as bad weather interfered.

While in Dickinson, I saw a WAAC walking smartly by on the sidewalk. I stopped painting and looked at her, as WAACs not being normal pedestrians on Dickinson streets. She eyed me coolly, not cracking a smile. I overheard a conversation between a soldier and his former employer not long ago. His opinion of WAACs was far from complimentary. He said the girls won't associate with the servicemen and keep away from them as though they were 'a specimen of poisonous reptiles,' or 'creatures out of the jungles of Africa.' They are not at all courteous or friendly. So that was the opinion of one GI. Perhaps WAACs have good reasons to be cautious of GI Joes. I am asking this question out of nothing more than curiosity.

Where was the school you taught last season located? I made a trip through the Killdeer Mountains a while back and passed several schoolhouses and wondered if one was your institution of learning. Is it the one near to where Banges live or the one west of Highway 22? It is beautiful and scenic country, but naming them mountains is kind of a misnomer. But it sounds impressive, so what the heck.

I'll have to agree that 'homemaker' is more befitting than 'housekeeper,' the latter sounding more like a 'hired maid' is another word that is used. I hope Lyla is happy being both. It is getting late, so I'll sign off for now. I enjoyed your very candid and informative letter and hope that it may be one of many. And I am sure the day will arrive when we will meet and visit in person. Bye for now. Sincerely, Raymond."

Letter Three from Marie

"Dear Raymond: Surprises in no small number. But then life today is just bundles of surprises opened at convenient times. Thanks a million for the grand picture. Nothing was said but I surmised that I could keep it. I would really like to. To be frank, it exceeded expectations. I never envisioned you as a creature from out of the jungles of Africa. Does your orchestra have a name? Just about the time one wants to see a *Killdeer Herald,* you can't find one. Either someone started a fire with it or it was sent to the neighbors. So I'm still in the dark. Will you enlighten the point at hand?

As for dances at Halliday, much and yet little can be said. The stores have open house on Wednesday and Saturday nights, so the town is jammed. On Saturday there is a show first. There used to be several dances a week. But now they are less often. No, I did not see the play the Grassy Butte young folks put on. Perhaps I was attending summer school.

We are having a heck of a time putting in a garden with a spade, rake and hoe. Our garden is far from small. We must be and are all out for victory. But rain has slowed the process. Should we complain? Heaven forbid! It's the only time one gets to rest and perhaps get in a few extra winks. It also gives farmers a chance to sit around and devise ways of spending all the money this downpour will fetch, all other factors being equal. We have started 28 varieties of Irises. Should they all bloom at one time it would be a sight to behold. Should they die, it would be likewise. The colors are mixed and of every kind.

Yes, we too have heard rumors of conditions out west. My aunt told me to bring a quart of cream if I came. They love old-fashioned vegetable soup and can't get any cream. They live in Spokane, so we can all imagine what conditions are on the coast proper. Just the same, I'd like to see it. The spirit of adventure cannot be subdued. The Mission begins on Ascension Thursday and ends the following Sunday. Good gracious, why should I mind if you should find yourself in Halliday? It would be a pleasure indeed. Do as you desire, and I'm positive you won't offend anyone. I await your arrival. Sincerely, Marie."

Meeting Marie, Finally!

One sunny Sunday afternoon in June 1944, the meeting between Marie and me came to be. I had written her a letter informing her that I would arrive at about 2 P.M. on this day. I drove slowly from Halliday to her house a mile west of the town, pondering what words to use to introduce myself. What impression would I make? "First impressions are lasting impressions," the saying goes. Would she take one look and tell me to get lost? I was quite nervous to say the least. What would she look like? I envisioned her at about 5' 8" and sort of a medium build. I did know she was a blonde.

The Commes house appeared up ahead. It was an older, modest, two-story structure. Good sign. The Commes were apparently on the same social level as the Schmidts. I was glad it was not a huge luxurious mansion, or I might have driven right on by. I stopped in the parking area and got out of the car. A petite-sized, brunette girl came out of the house and walked towards me. She must be Marie's younger sister, I thought to myself. She extends her hand: "Hello, I'm Marie. You must be Ray," she said, smiling sweetly.

"That I am. We finally meet. It's good to see you," I responded.

"Did you have a nice drive coming over?"

"Yes. I found your house without any trouble," I assured her. She had specs perched on her nose (like a Norman Rockwell painting of a country schoolmarm).

"Come in," she said, leading the way to the living room sofa. We sat side by side and talked small talk for a while. "My parents and family will be home soon. They went to visit Uncle Steve and Aunt Teresa this afternoon." I found this a bit odd, their leaving their daughter home alone with this Ray guy, a total stranger. Apparently they had no concerns. They came home shortly thereafter, and Marie introduced me to her family: mom Barbara, dad Frank, and sisters Evelyn, Ramona, and Kathleen.

Everyone was polite, sociable, and pleasant. Nice country folks they were. I was favorably impressed. Mother Barbara invited me to stay for dinner, which was delicious. Chicken and dumplings. She was a super good cook. It had been a pleasant afternoon, and I drove home feeling good about this new relationship. Marie and I seemed compatible, and I really liked her. But her small stature troubled me. Could a little woman like that safely have babies?

Marie beside the Commes family sedan, a 1936 Oldsmobile.

COURTING MARIE

After our first pleasant Sunday afternoon visit, Marie and I continued writing letters to one another. There was no texting in those days. We both decided we liked each other. She invited me to come again. I went to see her three weeks later, and we went to a movie. Later, we sat in the car and talked for hours about a variety of subjects, about our families, our likes and dislikes, unromantic stuff. We were just getting to know each other. On our third date we were holding hands at the movie. Then there was that first memorable goodnight kiss, her first, she said. We didn't pucker very well but improved with experience in the many that followed. There was no hanky-panky shenanigans in this romance. The stern teachings of our mothers and priests prevailed.

This is Marie (with hat and dog) at her Uncle Steve's house, when she was teaching at Big Flat country school in 1944 and boarding there.

The WLS-Radio National Barn Dance was coming to Dickinson. The Chamber of Commerce or somebody sponsored this show. The Barn Dance was a one-and-a-half hour radio program of music and comedy broadcast from Chicago every Saturday night. I was an ardent listener, and they were comin' to town. Whoopie!

I bought the first two advance tickets sold intending to take my sweetheart Marie to this high-class venue. But on the evening of the show my date Marie and I didn't get a seat. We arrived 15 minutes before the show to find the place packed and an angry crowd of ticketholders outside. "Tough luck." Not a great date, this.

Marie taught at Big Flat school south of Halliday for two years and stayed at her Uncle Steve and Aunt Theresa's house near the school. I would visit and pick her up from there. She remembers and likes to remind me of the time I picked her up and carried her across a mud puddle between the house and the car after coming home from a date. It was during the spring thaw. She hadn't worn her overshoes. We were in love. I proposed marriage to her in the car in front of her Aunt Kathryn's house in Dickinson, where she was staying while going to college. She said, "Yes, yes, yes!"

Marriage and a Honeymoon

Vows were exchanged between Ray and Marie on a beautiful sunny day: June 4, 1946. A small group of family members were present. Our attendants were my cousin Richard and Marie's sister Rosalie. God's representative was Father Francis Rehberg. A little cloud and light rain shower lasting less than a minute passed over as we came out of the church, "a sign that in this marriage would have very few tears," Father Rehberg prophesized.

The newlyweds with the reverend who tied the knot.

Following the ceremony was a dinner at the Halliday Hotel, a typical small town, three- story wooden structure with a restaurant operated by the owners, Mr. and Mrs. Jurgens. Mrs. Jurgens baked the best cherry pie. After dinner everyone went across the street to a nice city park and visited. The bride and groom later went to Dickinson for picture taking and then back the park. By evening we went back to Dickinson and spent the night at the Midwest Motel.

The next day we motored to South Dakota. The Black Hills in that state was a favorite honeymoon trip of that era. We visited Marie's Uncle John and Aunt Mary on our honeymoon. They lived at the foot of the Black Hills. I've never met a more fun couple. They insisted on driving us through the Black Hills, which they did, in three days. Uncle and me in the front seat. Marie and Auntie Mary in the back as we drove through the curvy roads in the hills. Here are some snippets between John and Mary:

Marie's Uncle John and Aunt Mary

Mary: *John, you're supposed to drive on the right side of the road, not the middle.*
John: *I know that, but when there's no cars coming, you can drive wherever you want on these curvy roads and save a lot of time and money by cutting them short.*
Mary: *It's only 14 and one-half miles to the top of Harney Peak.*
John: *No, it's not. It's only 14 and one-quarter.*
Mary: *No it's not. Just look at your speedometer. Besides. You shouldn't be going*

up here with a car. It's too steep for cars. It is for people on horses.
John: *Oh we'll make it.*

Halfway up Harney Peak, steam comes up from underneath the Plymouth's hood and it stops.

Mary: *See, I told you!*
John: *It will be OK in a few minutes.*

And it was. We managed to chug to the top of Harney Peak, and the view was spectacular in all directions. "Look south," said John. "We can see Nebraska. Ain't that something?"

Marie and I toured the Black Hills for three more days, looked at Mount Rushmore, but mostly at each other. Then we headed for home. It was time to get serious about making a living.

STARTING MARRIED-LIFE OUT ON THE FARM

My bride and I started our married life on my Grandpa Armbrust's farm, which we rented on a sharecrop deal. We paid Grandpa Armbrust one-quarter of the wheat crop. Fair enough. In the event of a crop failure, we both lost. Marie was a country gal, so farm life was no big jolt to her.

The old house was the first of several old junkers she had to contend with. There was no electricity or plumbing. A rather large metal tub for pre-soaking laundry doubled as a bathtub for adults and older kids. For the little kids, the smaller "face-and-hand" wash basin was used. This sat beside the water pail on a washstand in the utility room, which was refilled from two 10-gallon cans brought from the neighbor's well, as the Armbrust farm was devoid of a potable water supply. We hauled it from our neighbor Carl Roshau's well a quarter mile to the west of us, two 10-gallons cans per trip on the back of the pickup or the horse-drawn wagon or sled. The Roshau kids would insist on helping us pump, often two of them working the pump handle at the same time. Carl and Margaret had 14 beautiful, happy, well-mannered children. Carl loaned me machinery, and Margaret helped Marie with baby issues. A truly wonderful family they were. We will always love them. Years later they would stop and visit us when traveling through Montana, where we had moved.

We did have a well for watering livestock. It had a windmill for pumping. One windy day the wheel came loose and got bent up. I straightened it and climbed up the 30-foot tower to reassemble it while my pregnant young wife watched and fretted below, visions of early widowhood tormenting her.

We eventually bought a kerosene-powered refrigerator. Having cold milk and ice tea was a luxury. We also added a combination wood, coal, and kerosene range. Then of course there was the outhouse, a must-have structure for almost every rural farmstead. A favorite trick at Halloween was pushing it over. But I was a nice guy and never did that stuff.

The house had a large unfinished attic, providing Mickey and Minnie's mouse relatives room to frolic at night, which made it difficult for us to sleep. It was time to get a cat or two....

Becoming a Daddy

Our daughter Mary asked me one day, "Dad, where does Mother calling you Daddy come from? She refers to you always as 'Daddy.'" Well, Mary and others, let me tell you about that. Marie and I were walking along Main Street in Dickinson one sunny day about three months after we were married, doing a little shopping. She suddenly turned a bit pale and announced she felt very ill. We hurried to our nearby car and pondered the situation. Dr. Rodgers' office was nearby, so we decided to go there. In those days people went to the doctor when they were ill and not next Tuesday when you had an appointment. After her visit with the doctor, she came out of his examining room, sat down beside me, and murmured, "Nothing to worry about, Daddy."

I've been "Daddy" ever since. Raymond, Jr. was born ten months after we said "I do." He was an 8 pounder. This put to rest my fears about this little woman's ability to have babies.

Mr. Roshau was the president of a local school district in need of teachers. Upon discovering that Marie was a teacher highly recommended, he was determined to have her teach at Willmen No. 2, just down the road about a half mile from our house. She resisted. There was baby Raymond to care for. A plan was formed. Lillian Metz, who brought her children to the school, would take baby

Raymond home with her during the day and bring him back when school let out and she came to pick up her kids. Marie was reluctant but finally agreed. She knew all the kids in the community and liked teaching.

On days when Lillian was unavailable I took the infant with me to the field. I had built a cab on my tractor, which was an oddity, as there were no cabs on tractors then. So my son went round and round the field with me, sleeping in a comfy padded box beside Daddy, suckling on his bottle and binky. He did get a bit dusty though but didn't seem to mind it.

Upon hearing of her grandson's lifestyle, Marie's mother took immediate action, relocating the infant to the safety of her home near Halliday. We visited him on weekends. Marie's students all loved her, and the board begged her to continue teaching, but she declined, opting to be a full-time mommy. She desperately missed her baby.

Snowed in with a Baby Coming

New Year's Day 1949: Marie, me, and little Raymond attended mass in Dickinson and visited my parents. We also did some shopping, stocking up on groceries and other necessities. It was a good thing because it would be a while until we would shop again. It started snowing as we drove home, and it continued falling for several days until it had dumped 30 inches on the ground, paralyzing the entire region. Snowbound we were, big time. A breeze blew every day adding little drifts, like waves on a lake. A 50-mph wind creating a whiteout blizzard would have been more welcome. It would have piled this stuff up and into ravines.

Nothing moved. Ranchers could not feed their cattle, schools were closed, and mailmen dropped mail once a week from small planes. There were no snowmobiles or large rubber-wheeled tractors in those days. Some folks had 4x4 pickups, but these were useless in this much snow, which had a crust on it that was almost hard enough to support horses and people walking on it but not quite. They would break through and be belly deep in snow. It was horrible.

Sax Aviation, a small-plane dealer in Dickinson, equipped its fleet of planes with skis and began flying rescue missions. Anyone needing assistance was instructed via radio to spread coal dust or ashes in the form of a cross in the snow, visible from the air, by his or her houses where a pilot could land and take off. (Few people had telephones then.) Sax's planes were very busy airlifting sick folks and medical supplies as well as food. The U.S. Air Force was called upon to drop hay bales to stranded livestock. We were fortunate to have a large enough barn with a hayloft to shelter our small herd and the team of horses, so we were OK. Well . . . not quite. Marie was expecting, and the time was nearing.

On St. Valentine's Day, the first clear day since January 1, she announced "the time to go." Good timing. I hitched my team of big, strong mares to the sled, put in a bed of hay and straw, quilts and blankets, and tucked in Marie and Raymond. We then picked up Ralph Roshau, the neighbor's 12-year-old son to help us, and headed for Highway 22, seven miles distant, following a sled trail along hillsides and paths of least resistance without regard for property lines.

Three hours later we were at the highway, only to find it blocked. Marie's pains had subsided, so that was a relief. As we pondered our next move, a highway department snowplow approached from the north, plowing at about four miles per hour, with a long line of cars and trucks following it. Ralph flagged a car and explained our plight to Mr. Ficek, the driver, who kindly gave us a ride. We got into his car, and Ralph headed home with the team and sled. Three hours later we were at my parents' house in Dickinson. Thank you, Mr. Ficek, wherever you are.

How I Got My Pregnant Wife to the Hospital—in a Horse-Drawn Sled

While in Dickinson, awaiting the new arrival Marie and son Raymond, we would be living in the unfinished basement of my parents' house. Also living there besides my parents were my sister Rose, brother Andy, and my twin brothers, Matt and George. It was somewhat crowded, but we made do somehow.

I went to the food store the next day and bought a supply of groceries to assure my survival out on the snow-clogged prairie. There were no more pains or signs of an impending birth, so it would be OK for me to go home to the farm. Dad took me to Sax Aviation

Airfield, southwest of town. Sax had a ski-equipped fleet of 150 and 170 planes, along with pilots to fly snowbound rural folks in and out of town.

We loaded my groceries into a compartment behind the seat. I paid Jack Thomas, the pilot, $8 for the 20-mile flight, climbed into the cabin, buckled up, waved at Dad, and I was on my way home. I looked down at the eerie snow-swept landscape below, the country held in the grip of omni-powerful Mother Nature. We landed in a field east of the house, taxied up close, and unloaded the cargo in the snow. I asked pilot Thomas to come and pick me up on the following Wednesday afternoon to take me back to Dickinson and Marie, and he did. The nearest phone was at Charles Franchuk's house one mile south cross country. I would slog through the snow regularly to the home to call Dickinson and get a progress report from Marie. No news yet.

One night I was awakened at 2 A.M. by the sound of an engine running, and it wasn't a dream as I first thought. A Caterpillar was plowing the main east-west road. I lit the kerosene light and set it on the table by the window and watched. The driver of the Caterpillar saw the light, backed up, and plowed the road past the garage door to our house. I went out and invited him in and offered to cook coffee. He politely declined, saying he was with the U.S. Army and his destination was County Commissioner Carl Roshau's farm. Could I direct him there? The U.S. government had declared this a disaster area, and the Fifth Army was sent to help plow out roads, stranded cattle, haystacks, etc. I told him how to get to Carl's, and he thanked me. I thanked him for plowing out my car as he went by the garage door.

As soon as he was gone, I put coat and cap on, started the car, and was on my way to Dickinson at 4 A.M., in time to welcome into the world a baby daughter, who would be named Cynthia Susan. Mother and child were doing fine. Shortly after bringing the mother and new baby home, another snowstorm with wind blew in blocking the roads again. It was a hard winter.

Large Families: Don't Knock 'Em

There are times when it is uncomfortable to tell someone that you have ten brothers and sisters and/or eight kids. Some peoples' reaction is, "Oh my God," as though this were a disaster on the scope of a tsunami or a 9.5 earthquake. Others get the "Oh, that poor woman" expression. But most will be polite, smile, and say something like, "Oh, that's wonderful, that's great. Eight children, huh? How nice." What they are really thinking is, "Good grief, is that all they ever do is _____? (Insert your own word or sentence here.) That's another dumb bunch that will be on welfare for us hardworking taxpayers to support." I've heard it said and seen it in print many times.

So let me write a few observations in defense of large families. First of all, let's debunk the "dumb" moniker. I don't believe that. I grew up in and among large families, and their IQs were just fine. They became successful farmers, carpenters, businesspeople, nurses, doctors, musicians, teachers, etc., etc.

Following Pearl Harbor, two million guys, many of them from large families, volunteered for the military. Thousands of girls, including many from the Fayette community, headed for Boeing and the Portland, Ore., shipyards to become "Rosie the Riveter" types. These people kept us from being crunched by the Japanese.

Large families make things work in this democracy. They create households, which buy and consume goods, providing paychecks for tens of millions of people. Ray and Marie's eight kids and their spouses and their own kids maintain and pay taxes on a bunch of houses, own dozens of cars and trucks, pay buckets full of sales taxes, gas taxes, income taxes, state and federal, taxes on Miller Lite and Budweiser, taxes, taxes, taxes. Ray and Marie have contributed a real estate developer, some nurses, an engineer, an editor, artist, store manager, and teacher to the world. We helped fill the collection plates and the pews at our church, exchanging the peace, and holding hands while praying in unison with thousands of people. Most of them are sinners to some degree, as are we. Maybe some of them are illegal immigrants who came here to do the hard, dirty work.

So all of you one-and-two-kid parents, listen up: One day you could live in a country of senior citizens, like Japan, from what I am reading. All you will have is your money. The upside is, without enough young boys being born, there can be no army. So wars may become obsolete. Is that what you are striving for?

This is a picture of me and my "ginormous" family. I am the tall guy in the back. My wife, Marie, is standing next to me. The nun is my sister Lynn. Notice the two "angry" blonde toddlers in the middle of the photo. They are my twin brothers, Matt and George. My mother gave birth to them at the age of 48!

Two Action-Packed Years: The Story I Never Wanted to Have to Tell

This is a story of how I got myself into deep doo doo way back in 1951. You have probably heard the saying "curiosity killed the cat." You have also probably heard the saying "stay curious." I can add to this: "Curiosity can also get you tossed in jail!"

It happened to me. I am letting this skeleton out of the closet now at the urging of my family. Some of my family members know about it and may have their own versions from snippets they heard on the news or gathered from someone else. My children have been kept in the dark about it until now. So here is the true story. I've kept it a secret because I was ashamed that I did something so stupid. Now I am old and don't give a damn. And as far as I know, I'm the only one in the story who is still alive . . . at this writing anyway. So, read on.

After four crop failures due to drought, hail, and some other reasons, farming became discouraging. Why struggle and work and hope the weather sees fit to bless me with an income? I began thinking about a career change. Getting a good job, a regular paycheck, benefits, regular hours, a vacation with pay, days off. I wanted to live an orderly life like my city friends were enjoying.

Marie and I bought a house in south Dickinson for $3,000. Imagine buying a house for $3000. It was tiny and old and had no plumbing other than a cold water faucet and a one compartment sink in the little area used as a kitchen.

There was a living room and two tiny bedrooms. No bathroom. Nope, an outhouse back by the alley. We had three kids. So my Dad and I tore this house apart, salvaged the lumber and proceeded to build a new home on the site. As it neared completion I began thinking about looking for a job or a business. I needed to find a means of supporting my growing family.

A government job never entered my mind. The ad gave a date, time, and room number at the post office building in Dickinson. It didn't mention any educational requirements. Did a farmer with an 8th grade diploma from a country school have a chance of getting a post office job? Hardly. This would certainly be a job for educated city guys who had gone to high school and college.

But I could dream and wish. I would be working indoors out of nasty weather. No manure or oats to shovel. No ornery cows or horses to wrassle. No eight-mile sled trips through waist deep snow to the highway, or worrying about the possibility of babies being born in a two-horse open sleigh. Here in town I could drive to the hospital in a few minutes on a nice wide paved street, cleared of snow by city crews. This government job would offer benefits: A retirement pension, insurance, vacation with pay, regular hours, and the prestige of "working for the government." It was all so tempting. So, I decided to try for it. What the heck. Nothing ventured, nothing gained! On the day of the test, I walked in the door of room 210, very nervous and wondering what the hell I was getting myself into.

A woman who I will call "Fay" (I won't use real names in this story) directed me to a chair at a table, which was one of several. She was evidently prepared for more job applicants than just the two others besides me. One was a middle-aged guy about 55 wearing a suit and tie. The other was a younger man wearing military garb. As Fay explained, the passing grade was 70, but someone with military service could pass by scoring 60 on the test. There was a time limit in which to complete the questions, I think it was two hours. They were mostly multiple-choice questions on various subjects—zingers like, "How many states are there in the Union: 13, 48, or 36? If a person bought 10 three-cent stamps and paid with a ten-dollar bill, what would be the coins and bills for the correct change?" Stuff like that. I felt reasonably sure I had passed, But no scores were disclosed after the test.

Several days after the test, the post office called, and shortly thereafter I was sitting in the postmaster's office for an interview, nervous as a drowning cat. Fay was there. She was the assistant postmaster. The postmaster was a huge guy, about 6'-8" and weighed about 300 lbs., for sure. I'll refer to him as "Ace." He had a deep gravelly voice and was smoking a cigar. He extended his hand: "Hello Raymond. I'm glad to meet you," he said. "Are you related to the late Carl Schmidt who was the Dunn County commissioner?"

"Yes sir. He was my grandfather," I replied, wondering if this would effectively kill or enhance my chances of becoming a postal worker.

"He was the best friend I ever had," the postmaster said. "And if you're anything like him, you'll work out just fine. So I'm signing you on. I'm supposed to give these jobs to veterans, but have none on the roster right now." The fact that I got the job but was not a vet was a sticking point for some of my co-workers, most of whom were vets. There wasn't much I could do about that. I just hoped I could win them over eventually.

Ace was rarely in the main work area where the grunting and the goofing off were going on. Twice a month he made out the paychecks and placed them on a shelf next to the time clock outside his office door. Once a year he would ride with the rural mailmen, carrying a clipboard, observing, checking, scribbling notations, and drinking beer which the carriers brought with them on the route.

Fay explained the workings of the postal system. She assigned Martin V, an old WWI vet who had worked there for 30 years, to tutor me for several days. I paid attention to what Martin said and carefully stored all of it in my mind. My first shift started at 2 AM. My job was to the get mail for the Dickinson to the Williston, N.D. area loaded for its driver, John A. This included all the mail for the towns of Manning, Killdeer, Grassy Butte, and Watford City as well.

The Watford City bag included Arnegard and towns east and

west of it. This also included bulky items, parcels, and bundles of the Dickinson Press newspaper, which were delivered to the post office sometime during the night and left outside under the canopy of the loading dock. I had to drag them in, weigh them, and enter the weight on a form to determine the amount of postage. John had some hellish loads to deliver in the '49 Mercury four-door sedan he was using. (Post office personnel used their own cars back then.) He had a carrier rack on top and during the Christmas season this rig was a sight to behold. Martin helped me for three mornings and then gave me the keys to the post office. I was on my own. Good luck Ray! Live and learn. And so I did . . . did I ever!

Going to work at 2 AM and unlocking and entering a totally dark and empty post- office building is a spooky thing. You never knew who might be lurking nearby. A street light dimly lit the rear entrance steps, which admitted me to the loading area. Then the second interior door had to be unlocked. Inside, it was pitch black. I had to have a flashlight to make my way through the building. The heating system consisted of steam and radiators with the boiler in the basement. In the winter time these old systems banged and hammered. It was like a crew of plumbers pounding down there but I was too wimpy to go down 16 steps into that dungeon and investigate. Bud W, the city policeman on night duty, usually dropped by at about 3 AM to check and chat and read his mail. This helped calm my nerves. I was glad to see him, although it was against the rules to leave the door unlocked or let anyone in.

After getting John A on the road I busied myself working the sacks full of mail left by the previous crew, sorting it for the four city routes, the five rural routes, and the post-office box holders. First-class letters, "junk mail" letters, magazines, newspapers, parcel post, (packages) all had to be directed accurately to the proper "pigeon holes" and bins. The carriers expected accuracy or they would snarl and cuss at us "clerks" as we were called. I studied hard.

When I had all the work caught up, I would stand in front of the mailmen's racks of pigeon holes to learn who lived where. I had an edge on the rural routes as I knew where a lot of the farmers lived. I rode with the rural drivers whenever I had time.

During my two years at this government job, some unique events occurred. The staff was a wily bunch, and some were more motivated than others. You never knew what they would do---or not do.

My first task upon coming to work was to pick up the letters that during the night may have been mailed in the drop box on the sidewalk in front of the building. One night someone (maybe Mort) stuffed a big black cat into this mailbox. When I opened the side access door, this frightened beast bounded out, scattering letters all over the sidewalk and scaring the hell out of me.

Another heart-stopper was the cardboard man. The advertising geniuses for Seagram's whiskey created a life-sized cardboard man for their ads. Copies of him were placed in state liquor stores and bars around the country. He was a dapper grinning chap wearing a hat and smartly suited up. He was pointing a finger on one hand at a bottle of Seagram's finest hooch that he was holding in the other. Some smart ass (Mort again maybe?) got a hold of one of these cardboard dudes and placed him behind the lobby door. Mort, or whomever, had removed the hand holding the booze bottle. In the semi-dark, his finger looked like a gun pointing at you the instant you stepped through the back door of the post office. I unlocked and opened the door and geez! This had to be an inside job because the cardboard guy was inside between two locked doors. He didn't come in from the outside. After my heart resumed its normal rhythm, I brought Mr. Cardboard inside and stationed him out of sight just around the corner of the area where the rural carriers lined up their routes. Louie L, the Route 2 mailman, was the first to bump into him with an arm full of mail that morning. I heard a yelp followed by "Goddamn you, Shmitty."

Other entertainment of interest on my 2 AM shift was watching intoxicated patrons exiting the Esquire Lounge across from the post office. One farmer was a frequent patron at the Esquire as well as the Shamrock Bar up the street, depending on where he had not been tossed out of. Frequently he was clinging to the street lamp post with one hand, arms outstretched, reaching for the door handle of his truck parked across the street in front of the Woolworth's store, a daunting reach for anyone. He'd fall down, get back up, and hook one leg around the post, hoping to extend his reach enough to get a hold of that damn door handle. His hat had fallen off. He would take an occasional sip from a bottle in his pocket and scratch his head as he pondered his dilemma and planned his next move. It was like a W.C. Fields movie scene. (For those of you who are too young to remember W.C. Fields, think of a sloshed Will Ferrell, and you will get the picture.) Bud, the city night cop happened to drive by, noticed the farmer's futile efforts, and escorted him to a cot in the city jail for the night. Bud also presented him with a ticket for illegal parking.

One morning after groping for the light switch in the post office and turning it on, I found myself face to face with two scruffy looking burglars who were busily ripping open packages in the dark. Torn up packages were strewn around. We stood staring at each other. "What the hell are you guys doing here?" I blurted out. "May we ask the same of you?" one of them politely inquired.

I think they assumed they were caught in the act and were ready to be handcuffed and led away to a nice cot in jail and maybe given something to eat. "I work here," I said as I slowly backed away from them toward a shelf where Clarence, the general delivery man, kept a Colt .45 behind some boxes. Clarence had shown it to me. Apparently he envisioned the perils a 2 AM shift worker could encounter. I wouldn't have known how to use his Colt anyway. But the burglars fled out the back unlocked door I had just entered. I called the police department and Bud came screeching into the parking lot. "Where the hell were you this morning when I needed you?" I chided him.

To make a long story short: These were two drug-addled hobos looking for parcels addressed to the drugstore. They had broken a tiny window in the post office and crawled into it. It was a neat trick because the window was about 10 feet up from the sidewalk. One must have stood on the other's shoulders. The police found and apprehended two suspects asleep in the shade under a box car in the railroad yard. They had me come to the police station and identify them. One was sitting on the toilet, nonchalant as could be. A judge sentenced them to do time in a federal prison because messing with the U.S. post office is a federal offense. *The Dickinson Press* sent a reporter to interview me for the story. I got my name in the paper. (It would appear there again, many times.)

I continued to do the 2 to 10 AM shift for almost a year. Their first year new employees are called "subs." It's kind of a probationary period. No regular hours. Fay called me whenever she was in a bind. She worked the hell out of me, but aside from the crazy hours, this job was "a piece of cake" compared to stacking hay and shoveling grain and coal.

I was trained to work every station in the entire operation except the money order window. I seldom went home at the end of my shift at 10 AM. I made a bunch of money with all the overtime and bought a new Dodge Coupe. The last crew of the day shift would leave sacks full of junk mail and magazines and parcel post for me to sort on my early morning shift. Mort would come in early to line up his route. He'd glare at me. "Work, you draft-dodging SOB" was maybe what he was thinking. But he realized that I sorted his mail correctly, which made his job easier, so I didn't think he minded my being there, veteran or not.

Fay handed me a chart one day. "Ray, you have to learn and memorize this," she said. It was a schedule of all the mail carrying trains in North Dakota. For example: Northern Pacific Mandan to Killdeer Lv Mandan at 1:15 PM, Ar Killdeer 6:10 PM Mon. thru Fri. Fargo to Ellendale, Mandan to Mott, and so on. Who needs this? There were about 50 of these branch lines in the state. I had to learn and memorize them all. It helped me sort mail more accurately. Bob, one the carriers, would come in, see me and yell, "Oh good. Smitty is working. The mail will be right this morning."

I rode with the carriers and learned the routes too. Bob and Louie L were hunters and took their .22 rifles with them and shot rabbits along the way. They would then stop at Dickinson Hide & Fur to sell them before returning to the post office, I would drive their routes for extra money when they took days off. I bought and used a yellow Jeep.

I also carried a foot route from time to time. Bill S, a regular carrier would get really thirsty when he neared the Mint Bar. So, he would stop in to remedy this problem. His friends there insisted on buying him beers, for which he was grateful and couldn't refuse. After a while the phone at the post office would ring and I would be called to finish his route. So I've been a rural and city mailman. I also learned to deliver parcels to homes. Frank L was my teacher. Frank slung packages on the porches and steps without notifying the recipient. It was the easy way to do it but not the best. We delivered lots of items to a wholesale grocery place, tossed them outside the warehouse door, and drove off.

"You don't have to lug that crap inside," Frank instructed me. The grocery manager would call the postmaster mad as hell, and he chewed our butts. I feared he might regret hiring me. Frank was unfazed. He kept doing it his way. I found out later that he was

Mort's nephew and not a vet either. Mort seemed OK with that.

I was getting a little scared that this job was hazardous to my life because of the number of deaths in my two years there. Many of my coworkers drank a lot—at least one of them to death, I believe. Maybe it was from the trauma of having been in the military. I don't know. Another died in a fire, a third in an auto accident. Murray D was one of my favorite coworkers. A diplomat, teacher, and advisor to me, he could calm the most irate postal customer. He ended up hanging himself. Carl S contracted multiple sclerosis and died, leaving a bunch of kids. Carl was a fighter to the end, carrying mail as long as he could stagger. Not knowing he had multiple sclerosis, people would call the post office complaining about the "drunk" mailman.

I survived my first year without getting fired or killed. A new guy took my thrill-packed 2 AM shift, and I trained him. He was a college grad and kept reminding me of it. I told him I graduated from the school of hard knocks. He looked puzzled when I said that.

I now was in the "permanent appointment" league, which meant I had a job for life working only 40 hours a week. I got vacations with pay, days off, and would get retirement pay after 30 years of stamp canceling and pigeon holing zillions of letters and junk mail.

The shorter hours gave me more time to work on our new house. Marie, the kids, and I were living in my parents unfinished basement during construction, so I hurried to get us moved into the new home, which was a small, two-bedroom, 800 sq. ft. house with a full basement. Finishing part of the basement seemed the fastest and the least costly. This project up to now was a pay as you go. I could work on the upstairs while we lived in the basement. So that's how we proceeded.

I was now assigned the closing 10 PM shift. The lobby was to be locked at 9 PM. I went through the same ritual doing this as the morning one but in reverse. But now I had lights on while working the locks. I liked this better.

One night just before locking up I heard someone put a letter in the drop box in the lobby. A brown sedan drove away from the front of the post office afterward. I went outside and gathered the mail out of the "cat" mailbox and went back inside, locking the doors as I went. Then I went to get the mail from the drop box in the lobby. There was one letter in it. I canceled the stamp and put it into its pigeon hole. It was addressed to Charles K, a farmer I knew from the area where we had lived. I had been in his house and visited him once with another one my neighbors. Charles was remodeling the interior and showed us around. He was a cordial man.

I had all the mail sorted and put on the carrier's desks—all but this last mailed letter. I started to sort it for its route and noticed that the return address was sort of odd: PO Box 1050. There was no name on the envelope, just a box number. It was neatly typed. I took it to the box area, and looked around. There was no PO box 1050. This was strange. A nonexistent post office box. How intriguing . . .

The general delivery desk had a light that illuminated the contents of envelopes to some degree. Clarence used it, not for spying on people's mail, but in an effort to maybe see names or addresses or clues that would be useful for delivery in the event of damage to the addresses or names on the outside of packages and envelopes. I held Charles K's letter up to it and read the beginning of an extortion plot. The writer claimed he knew that Charles had filed a fraudulent tax form. For a sum of money the writer would hush up about it. The letter was folded so the rest of it was doubled up and I couldn't read it.

Chuck H was backing up to the dock with a few sacks of mail. We unloaded it, and he was on his way to his rural route. I hurriedly processed the newly arrived mail and went back to the letter. It was lightly sealed. The temptation was great and my curiosity overwhelming. I opened it . . . big mistake. And a crime.

The writer claimed he had knowledge *and* proof that Mr. Charles K had cheated on his tax return. The amount demanded was $750 or $1,000. I don't remember exactly. This hush money was to be placed in a rural mailbox south of town. The letter described the mailbox, the name on it, and that it was on the right side of the highway. The letter also designated the date and time the drop was to be made.

As I was reading this, Louie L came in the back door as he often did to arrange his mail for the next day. I handed him this letter. He read it and said, "Holy s---. Did you open this Ray? Seal it up and put it back in the mail and don't tell another soul about it, or you'll get your ass fired." (Good advice. I should have taken it.)

Next, Henry K, an energetic, livewire mailman came bouncing in. "Watcha you guys got there that's so interesting?" he asked. It was too late to hide the letter as he would have seen us do it. Louie hands him the letter. Henry reads it and busts out laughing. He tosses the letter in the nearby wastebasket. "We'll go out and catch that punk," he says. "I don't think Charlie will pay anyway. This is bullshit." The discussion went on for a while. After Henry left, I retrieved the letter, resealed it with a little glue from a bottle on Clarence's desk and put it back in the mail. The glue was later analyzed and this pointed to me as the letter writer.

Henry also worked part time at a gas station. He couldn't keep a secret and soon the story made its way around all of the employees, including Laudie F and Cap W, as well as John D. Plans were formulated among them to drive out there on the night of the drop and intercept this extortionist.

I wasn't sure I wanted any part of this action, but I was curious to see what happened. (Recall what happens to curious people.) So Monday evening at about 8:30, I parked on a side street near a street lamp and watched cars driving south on the highway out of town. Shortly thereafter Henry pulled up behind me, stopped, and got into the passenger seat beside me. We didn't see Charles or anyone else of interest drive by. At about 9:15 he suggested driving south to see if anything was going on. So we did. As we neared the mailbox, Henry told me to stop at the box. I did. He rolled down the window, reached out, opened the mailbox, and retrieved an envelope. I protested and told him to leave it and asked him what he planned to do with it. He replied, "Send it back to Charlie."

By now Laudie F and Cap W were beside us in Laudie's Oldsmobile. As I started slowly driving away from the mailbox, a car came speeding from over a nearby hill. It pulled up abreast of me. It was a dirty black Ford sedan. The windows were rolled down and several handguns were pointing at us. So now we were dealing with a gang of dangerous bandits here, not just some punk? The shabby Ford had no markings or flashing lights or siren. It was just a plain dirty car. We had no idea that it was actually part of an FBI stakeout, or "sting."

Apparently there were one or more agents with radios hiding in tall weeds and grass in the ditch near the mailbox who signaled the FBI guys in the car behind the hill. My mind flitted to my pregnant wife at home and the likelihood of her becoming a young widow with four kids if I didn't stop and surrender the ransom. So I slowed down and stopped. Henry, the coward, opened the passenger side door, bailed out and ran into a cow pasture, disappearing into the darkness with the envelope. I guess it was now to be every man for himself. Laudie, now in front of me, put the pedal to the metal. The car was equipped with a high-performance "Rocket V8" engine. Rubber burned and screeched. The dirty Ford now abandoned me and focused on the speeding Olds. It was no contest. Laudie was pursued all the way to New England, N.D., a small town about 20 miles away. Then Laudie eluded the Ford by ducking into a residential area. He then turned back on the highway toward Dickinson. But the FBI agents must have noted his license number. Upon returning from the failed chase, they found and staked out his apartment.

I made a U turn and drove home, put my "hot" car in the garage, and went into the house and told my frantic confused wife that there was a problem and I had to go somewhere, but I'd be back shortly. I didn't want to engage a gang of gun-slinging extortionists at my house.

It was about 10:30. I ran to the Mint Bar, four blocks from my house, hoping to find someone of this trio there. I saw the hot Oldsmobile parked at the curb. The Mint was a popular old corner bar and a hangout of the working class. I entered and joined Laudie and Cap in a booth and we discussed our dangerous predicament. About now Henry comes in as well. He had run to his brother's farm. His brother gave him a ride back to town. We decided to go to Laudie's apartment to plan a strategy for our survival as these gunslingers may be looking for his car. His basement apartment entrance was in the rear of the building. There was a secluded parking spot among other cars. They wouldn't find it there.

As the four of us neared the apartment door, which was slightly ajar, Laudie's wife screamed from inside, "Don't come in! It's a trap. They got guns!" We scattered every direction through the lilac bushes and over garbage cans. Gunfire rang out through the night air as they fired rounds into the air behind us, bullets zinging over our heads. Then one of them shouted, "Stop! This is Matt Z, the chief of police!"

"Whoa! What's this?" I thought to myself. I knew the chief and this was his voice. It was a welcome one, on this night anyway. Charles K had notified authorities when he received the letter. They staked out the mailbox, and we four dumb self-appointed vigilantes stumbled right smack dab into their trap. All the while we thought we were trying to get away from gun-wielding big time bandits.

We four captured suspects were arrested and escorted into a room in the Stark County Courthouse and interrogated separately in different rooms by each "G-man" (FBI agent). They were trying to get a coherent story. There were six of them on this case. Four in the Ford, and two in the ditch by the mailbox. The questioning started as a casual conciliatory chat—like this was no big deal and they just wanted us to tell them why we did what we did. "Were you in financial trouble and needed money? Not to worry. Nothing much will come of this," they promised.

But each session by each G-man got progressively nastier. The last guy resorted to a form of torture in his effort to extract a confession from me. He was a big mean brute. He slammed my face against the wall, twisted my arm around my back, gripped my middle finger and bent it back, and kneed me in the crotch. "Talk, ya cheap small-town crook. Ya wrote that goddamn letter, didn' ya?" he said.

"No I didn't." I wailed." The middle finger got bent a bit more. "Didn' ya?" Another knee kick in the crotch, "Didn' ya? Didn' ya, ya cheap petty SOB," he snarled. "Didn' ya? Didn' ya?"

It went on and on. At this point I quit answering. I remembered the old saying: "You can talk yourself into trouble easier than out of it." I clammed up. I didn't say another word to him. He was pissed. "You're gonna rot in jail, you SOB," He told me before give up.

We four accused, alleged extortionists spent what was left of the night in separate jail cells. The next morning, one of the FBI guys and a postal inspector, as well as Otto T, a bargain-basement lawyer in town, escorted us to Judge Norbert M's chambers. "All right, you birds. How do you plead?" Otto commanded.

Judge M listened in silence to this bizarre story. And promptly dismissed it, except for the letter opening. He told lawyer Otto there was no other crime committed that could be successfully prosecuted. It would be a waste of time. Henry, Laudie, and Cap were free to go. But I was charged with tampering with the mail. The post office inspector asked me to hand over my post office keys. He escorted me to another room for a lie detector test. He told me I was lying through my teeth. My mailman career was over. I was fired from my first real "job." I was released to await formal charges. I walked 15 blocks home to face my confused frantic wife. It was the worst day of my life.

A policeman and a U.S. Marshall later came to the house and

picked me up to escort me to Bismarck to be charged with the crime of tampering with the mail. It was a federal offense. A felony. We went to get on the train. "I'm supposed to handcuff you, but I won't do that," the Marshall said. I was thankful for that.

He was an older polite gentleman dressed in a suit and tie instead of a lawman's uniform. We had a nice ride. I told him my story. He listened and wished me well. When I got to Bismarck, I was locked in a large cell in the Federal building. I shared it with an accused murderer who was a young Indian kid about 18 years old. He had been involved in a barroom brawl and a rancher beat him up real bad. In revenge he got his rifle out of his pickup, went back in the bar and shot him. My other cellmate was Richard D, a white middle-aged guy. He was charged with selling booze to the Indians. This was illegal. He was married to an Indian woman.

My two cellmates spent their time "Indian wrasslin'" on the floor. It's a sport like arm wrestling, only you do it with your legs instead of arms. They invited me to join the competition but I declined. I could have beaten the Indian kid, but not Richard. Mostly I looked out the window through the bars at the traffic three stories down.

Two days later my dad and father-in-law came and bailed me out. They posted a $4,000 bond. We drove home to Dickinson.

My good neighbor Amos F came running over to my house all excited when he saw I was home. "I'm reading this story in every paper in the state, and I don't believe it. Hell. You've been set up Ray. Are you sure you didn't get railroaded out by somebody over at the post office who doesn't like you? Maybe by some of your coworkers who were mad you weren't a vet?" I told him I had no idea.

Amos recommended the attorney Mr. M. "If this thing gets to court, he's the best man to have by your side," Amos assured me. I went to Mr. M's office for advice and guidance. He was a very handsome man about 60 years old. He had thick white hair that was neatly combed, and he was flawlessly dressed. An impressive looking lawyer. His advice: Plead guilty, throw myself at the mercy of the court, and hope for a light sentence. To fight this would be futile and would cost thousands of dollars. He would go to Bismarck with me and speak in my behalf. We would talk about the fee later.

A letter arrived with the date I was to appear. I picked up Mr. M at his house and we started down the two-lane highway toward

Bismarck. Occasionally he suggested we stop for a drink, so we did. I opted for Coke. He tipped a couple of loaded ones here and there and talked incessantly about not ever wanting to get married again—and the women he met who did. I was getting worried my legal advisor was getting sloshed and that he would stand in front of a judge who would abhor such conduct and throw the book at me: "Ten years of hard labor, Schmidt!"

We entered the courthouse and Mr. M looked for and found the men's restroom. He emerged five minutes later looking like a model right out of a store window. His hair was neatly combed, and he was dressed up to the hilt. He had taken along a garment bag and changed clothes.

We walked into His Honor's chamber right on time to the minute and looking good. The judge asked lots of questions, glanced up at my dapper attorney, cleared his throat, and asked, "How does the defendant plead?"

"Guilty, your honor," said Mr. M.

His Honor looked at me. "I will put you on probation for three years. Fill in one of these forms every month so we know where you are at and what you are doing, and send it to the probation office." He handed me a large brown envelope. "Now go home and take care of your family and don't let me see you here again. I'm quite sure I won't."

"Thank you, your Honor," I stammered.

"You're welcome," he said. "Next case."

Mr. M and I had a quick lunch at Danny's Drive Inn or whatever and drove home without stopping. It was getting dark and Marie would be worried.

I should have gone to Charles K's house and apologized for the incident, but I was too wimpy. A former neighbor of mine told me that Charles K shared the FBI's opinion that I was the letter writer and extortionist, and he was pretty damn mad at me. I'm sorry, Mr. K.

So this is the story. It was on the front page of every newspaper in the state of North Dakota. My dubious claim to fame. Had I not been curious, I would likely have been a retired postal worker who played cards with a bunch of old cronies at the Dickinson Senior Center.

Sometime later when Marie and I and our children lived at

Fayette, two smiley, friendly chaps drove up in a jeep to where I was repairing a fence. It turned out they were a couple of my old postal colleagues. They looked somewhat surprised to see me. Then they respectfully asked for permission to hunt deer on my land. I let them. There's no point in holding a grudge, is there?

That's my story, and I'm sticking to it.

How I Learned the Fine Art of Home Building

After the post office fiasco, I obviously needed a job. I got a tip from Leonard Scherger, a Texaco station operator, that a customer of his, a carpenter named Howard Steffes, was looking for a man. But Leonard warned me Howard was not an easy guy to work for. He was demanding and impatient. "Fires men at the drop of a hat," Leonard said, "When in a rage, nobody works for him very long." This wasn't good, but I needed a job.

I found Howard at Dr. Guillion's house working alone, on a three-story-plus-attic mansion. Howard was not very big. He was only about 5'8" but all muscle. He glared at me. "Who have you worked for?" he inquired. I informed him that I had moved in from a farm and had no experience.

"OK. $1.25 an hour, and come at 8 in the morning. No need for tools," he said, as he had extra.

Howard and I got along well. He worked very fast, and I made an effort to keep right up with him. He liked that. Mrs. Gullion invited us in for coffee and cookies every day at 10 AM and at 3 PM, during which time Howard and I got acquainted with each other. He was fascinated by my music activity and had many questions about the band, as his daughter aspired to be a singer. We worked at the Gullion's for eight months, redoing the entire house from the basement to an electric train room in the attic.

Howard had a brother, George, who had a busy cabinet shop doing kitchen and bath cabinets. So I got to spend time in George's shop making doors to match the paneling at the Gullion's and watching how cabinets were being constructed. The Steffes brothers were well-educated.

In various towns, Howard and I framed houses, each with complex rooflines, a challenge he loved and had mastered with the help of a steel carpenter's square. In Bismark, N.D., we stayed in an old downtown flophouse hotel with a shared bathroom. He prayed the rosary before going to sleep.

I quit Howard at the end of the summer and went to work for Little Joe (more about Joe next). Howard died at age 45 with a hammer in hand while building a house with a complicated roof line.

My Favorite Boss: Little Joe

Joe Ziegler, lumberyard manager, was one of the favorite people in my life. He was an individual like no other. He was my boss for the two years when I went to work at the Occident-Peavey Lumber Yard on Main Street in Dickinson.

What a character! Joe was a little guy, about 5-feet tall, if that. He had a hearing impairment and used a hearing device that consisted of a plug in the ear with a lead to an iPod-sized amplifier in his shirt pocket. He of course disliked answering the phone and had me do it whenever possible. But when he answered it, he held the phone against the amp thing in his pocket and shouted down at it.

Joe was good for a laugh a day, and yet it was so frustrating, it could drive me up a wall. He had these quirky ways of doing things. For example: One morning he comes bouncin' out of his office, "S*h*ay Ray (he added an *h* after the *s*), I'm going to the posht office to buy some shtamps. Joe then gets in his '47 Plymouth, a gift from his daughter, and drives to the post office, three blocks away. He parks in the 5-minute zone, starts up the steps, meets someone, and the two talk for an hour.

He then walks back to the lumberyard, tells me about his visit, fumbles through his pockets, and says, "Shay Ray. You know what? I forgot the shtamps." He then walks back to the post office, past his car, buys the stamps, and then walks back to the lumberyard and proceeds to stamp a bunch of envelopes. Next, he announces he is going to take them over and mail them, again walking past his car twice.

At lunchtime Joe peers at the lumberyard's parking lot. "Shay, Ray. You know what? Somebody shtole my car!"

"No, Joe," I reply. I think you'll find it at the post office in the 5-minute zone. Get in my car and I'll give you a ride over there."

Joe's driving was less than coordinated. His car had a stick shift, which was too complex for him to master. So, he simplified the process by starting and staying in second gear, being careful not to get into a situation where reverse would be needed. I rode with him several times. Being of short stature, getting his foot on the starter presented the first problem, as he was so short and the starter was at the far end of the floorboard. Not hearing was another problem: "Shay Ray, has it shtarted yet?" he would ask. "The only way I can tell is if them little needles shtart wiggling on them clocks on the dash."

We start with a lurch as he releases the clutch with the petal to the metal in second gear, headed for the Smiths' place. They weren't happy about the crappy two planks Dick, the yardman, had delivered them. Dick said he had dug through the whole stack looking for clear ones, but one had a small knot in it. It was the best he could do. "The Smiths are mad as hell, you talk to them," said Dick. That's where Joe and I are headed. Joe careened out onto Main Street without stopping or looking. He came to a stop at the traffic light two blocks away.

"Go, Joe. It's green," I say.

"Oh hell. I shtop if it's green or red or purple or brown, or whatever. I always shtop at a light," he replied. (I was told later that he was colorblind.) We get to the Smiths. The two planks were lying next to the small one-car garage in the alley. It had a dirt floor with a 1931 LaSalle sedan parked in it. The planks were to park this car upon. Mr. and Mrs. S came out of the house, calling Joes attention to the knot. "Not acceptable," they say. "We asked for no knots, and look what that kid brought up here! What kind of help do you have down there anyway?" Mrs. S asked.

"Shay, by golly. I'll have him come pick these up and refund your money, and you go to Heaton Lumber and buy your planks from them," Joe says. We start for the Plymouth.

"Oh no, we wouldn't think of going anywhere else. Maybe if we can get a discount for that knot?" the Smiths protest. So Joe gave them a dollar off, and the knotty plank was OK for the LaSalle.

One day two old cronies of Joe's who hung around the St. Anthony Club, a fraternal group of German immigrants, came in to buy shingles for a small house and needed a price (low) and advice on how to put on these damn new kind of asphalt shingles. The cronies were used to cedar. "Shay, you two old plugs got no business up on a roof," Joe warned. They told him to mind his own. "Ask Ray, how to put them on," retorted Joe.

"What the hell does that kid know?" they barked back. I instructed them as best I could: "The three tabs are the exposed part and go down."

"Oh bulls---t," replied one of them.

When Dick went to pick up the leftover bundle and some scraps for which they wanted credit, he said they had put the shingles on the roof upside down.

Joe couldn't hear so well, but he could add a column of numbers by sight faster than an adding machine. His mind was way ahead of his pencil, so it was a while before I was able to read his memos. They were sort of a shorthand all his own. He left out half the words. Many more stories could be told about this colorful individual "Little Joe Blow," as he was known. He was called this because he filled his cheeks and exhaled through his mouth. I was told by doing that, it opened his eardrum and he could hear better.

Joe was totally honest and truthful and showed respect for everyone, especially me. I will remember him as a mentor and a best friend. Joe was at this job for 55 years and had zillions of customers, but he didn't make much profit for the Peavy Lumber Co., according to their numbers anyway. He was a poor bill collector and was selling lumber at low prices to meet the competition.

Buying My Dream Farm, Fayette

In the spring of 1957, I left Occident Peavy Lumber and my favorite boss, Joe Ziegler. Wages of $265 a month didn't make ends meet. Joe's attempt to get a raise from the Occident Peavy's home office in Minneapolis was futile. My favorite childhood haunt and, in my opinion, the prettiest spot on planet earth, Fayette, was abandoned, with the exception of one person: Annie Fisher still lived in the stone house with Oscar, the bull snake who hung out there, controlling the mouse population.

The store at Fayette was closed, the land not leased, buildings collapsing. It was a real fixer-upper and right up my alley. But it had not been advertised for sale. So, Marie and I went for a Sunday drive, and I decided to pay Annie a visit. She was gracious but hesitant about selling. This had been her home for almost her entire life. She had inherited the 640 acres from Mr. and Mrs. Little, and parting with it appeared to be an emotional ordeal. But she was getting old and was alone there.

I asked for a price. After much silence, she timidly suggested $25 per acre, with $4,000 down, and the balance paid in $1,000 annual payments yearly at a rate of 4 percent interest. So that's how we bought Fayette. Annie reluctantly moved into an apartment in Dickinson.

Marie was not happy at Fayette. She would have to leave her new home in Dickinson and move into an old worn-out, stone house built in 1896. The house lacked adequate plumbing and electricity. The kitchen had an old coal-and-wood-burning stove to cook on and a rusted-out iron sink with almost no water pressure. She saw Fayette as fraught with hazards and dangers to her numerous children, with the river near the house, an old bridge, and timbered ravine nearby. There were old, open abandoned wells, a dozen tumbledown buildings, a sod store about to cave in, wildlife, skunks, coyotes, snakes, raccoons, foxes, and an array of hazards to threaten and endanger her bunch of kids. She was justified in her concerns and unhappy. I should not have done this.

The children liked Fayette, though. There were lots of very interesting places to explore, like the root cellar, a cold, dark, damp underground "dungeon," which served as a walk-in refrigerator for produce. Then there was the "Peaceful Valley," as they named it: A timbered, shaded ravine with a spring-fed rivulet bubbling along, making its way to the river. The Peaceful Valley was fragrant with wild fruit blossoms of many colors and all kinds of birds singing and chirping their own brand of music and messages. It offered a serene setting for a Sunday afternoon stroll.

An industrious explorer, a beaver, also liked the valley. The beaver would leave his clan and migrate up and dam the stream near the spring, which supplied our water. But I was in no mood to share it, so I kept ripping out his dams until he got discouraged and left. I'm sorry, beaver!

Betsy the Dog:
Our Guardian on the Farm

Betsy was a dog. She was the guardian of Fayette, keeping it clear of coons, coyotes, and all other undesirable varmints who might have a tendency to intrude. A German shepherd of top-notch breeding she was—smart, big and strong. Perfect for a dangerous a place like Fayette. There were lots of places for Betsy to explore, cows to chase, and children to play with. She would go with me to the fields and cow pastures, helping manage the herds, trotting alongside the farm machinery, detouring if something of interest caught her fancy, like chasing, but never catching, jackrabbits.

I was raking hay one day on a field by the river when I noticed Betsy at the water's edge, nose to nose with a raccoon in the water. I stopped and watched the most savage in-the-water fight ever. Betsy was on the bank and snarling. The coon was in the water, taunting her, luring her as if saying, "C'mon, c'mon. Jump in." And Betsy did, in spite of my yelling, "Betsy! No!"

What followed was hard to watch: two creatures fighting to kill and survive, the coon having an advantage in this water arena. They disappeared under the water, resurfacing, churning, and biting. Each was going for the jugular. This battle went on and on. It looked like I was losing my dog, and there was nothing I could do but watch.

But the coon was weakening, and Betsy thankfully prevailed. She dragged her defeated foe up on the hayfield and proceeded to chew, starting at the front to the rear, breaking every bone in the dead coon's body, flattening him out till he resembled a rug. Then she sat, trembling and snarling, daring him to move. I finished raking and went home, leaving her sitting there. She came home at sundown, several hours later when she was satisfied that Mr. Coon was no longer a menace to the community of Fayette.

But another potentially serious menace did come by. An apparently rabid skunk came loping along one day, joining the kids who were playing in the yard. Mother rounded up everyone, including Betsy, into the house. I went for the shotgun and made a call to the county's animal-control agent. One sign of rabies is lack of hair on an animal's tail. This stinker had none and had crawled under a building. I laced three eggs with strychnine and shoved them under there, blocking the entrance with stones. Later, the inquisitive Betsy, sniffer that she was, pawed the stones aside, and was able to reach and eat one of these poison eggs.

Betsy was lying in the yard, presumably sleeping and enjoying the summer afternoon, which she did often when she had everything under control in Fayette. Later, my daughter Mary called Betsy to fetch the cows, but she never responded.

Baby Julie and a Life-Changing Tragedy

This is the story of a blessed event during which something that went very wrong. Following a normal birth, a sweet, healthy, blonde, baby girl was born to me and my wife in 1959. She was our seventh child. There were no complications or problems; mother happy, dad proud, and brother and sisters awaiting the baby's arrival home.

The name for the new sister had been selected. She was to become "Julie Eva," sort of after my godmother, Mary Eva. A baptism was arranged for the following Sunday. Most of us went to Mass that Sunday, after which came the ceremony of the baptism. Julie Eva was now a Catholic. Her mother didn't attend the christening as she didn't feel well. When we got home, she was in bed. She told me to give our newborn to Marian, my sister, and for me to take care of the kids as she wasn't going to survive whatever this was. We put her into the car and sped to the Dickinson hospital 40 miles distant.

Mother's doctor (Dr. Rodgers) examined her and suspected a brain aneurysm. Nothing could be done for her condition, he said. However, there was a "specialist" in Fargo who might be able to help. But getting her there would be tricky. She would have to stay in a lying-down position.

Dr. Rodgers suggested using a special hospital car on the Northern Pacific (NP) railroad. I called the NP and was told the car was in Seattle or somewhere. The person I talked to wasn't sure. (It turned out later that the car went through Dickinson, right when we needed it.) Dr. Rodgers then suggested using a station wagon. I didn't know anyone who had one. However, the Dodge Dealer, Eddy Rakowski, had a used Ford station wagon on his lot. I told Eddy my story. He didn't want to lend it to me for liability reasons. Instead he sort of sold it to me. "Pay for it whenever you can," he said. (It took me five years to do that.)

The hospital staff in Dickinson helped bed down Mother Marie in that Ford, and the two of us headed for Fargo, about 300 miles to the east. I will leave out some of the details of the weeklong sojourn to Fargo. In a nutshell: The medics there said there was "nothing to do [for Marie] but for her to stay horizontal, move as little as possible, for weeks or months, and hope for the best. A normal lifetime was not likely but remotely possible," a depressing thing to hear. Many relatives came to help us. We are forever grateful to all of you. Marie spent 12 weeks in bed at Fayette, slowly gaining strength, while Marian nurtured the infant, Julie Eva. Mother and child were deprived of some bonding time during this critical time.

Maimed

Ouch! Accidents are common on farms. I had a profound one in 1959. I lost the tips of two middle fingers on my left hand. It was butchering and sausage making time at the Fayette farmhouse. The floor was littered and slippery with fallen meat scraps. I reached for a heavy distant kettle, lost my balance and grabbed at something to keep from falling. The running meat grinder. Bad move. It separated two middle fingers at the first joint. My first thought at that very second was not the pain, but of not being able to play music. Gone in an instant. Horrible trauma.

Of course, everyone sprang into action after my fingers had been ground off. They wrapped my hand up in bandages and my brother Jerome, who, along with his wife, was helping us with butchering, drove me to the hospital in Dickinson, some 40 miles away. It was a nice ride in Jerome's new Ford station wagon, but I didn't enjoy it very much.

I spent the night at the hospital. The next day, an insurance salesman who was always trying to sell farmer's disability coverage came to my room to persuade me to buy his products. Jerome ran him off.

So what happened to my fingers? With today's technology, they could have been sewn back on. But not back then. I seem to recall my sister-in-law saying she buried them. My oldest son, Ray, doesn't recall it that way. He cleaned the grinder and says he threw them in a field. My oldest daughter, Cindy, thinks she fed them to pigs while dumping what had been ground up. pigs. If that's so, I'm sure they loved it. It might even be kind of fair. After all, we were eating them all of the time. Now it was their turn to eat me.

You may be wondering if the loss of my fingers "killed" my accordion career. It didn't. My accordion career was pretty much over before then. After Marie and I married, we began having children (a total of eight). I continued to play the accordion to earn extra money. Meanwhile, she was home alone with all these kids while my band mates and I drove around the countryside to gigs—often on icy roads in the dead of winter. Usually a bit of hooch had been consumed.

This was not going to work with a family. I had to make a choice. It was not an easy one or one that Marie and I agreed on right away. I put the accordion down and it remained parked in our closet for years. Kinda sad, but true. Eventually I took it out and began playing for fun again. My youngest child, Amy, who was about six or seven years old at the time, was shocked by the sight. She had never before laid eyes on that accordion or her dad playing it.

Fayette, a Failure (Sort Of)

After three hailouts and a drought year, I was in arrears on my $1,000 annual payments to Annie Fisher. She wasn't pushing for payment, fully realizing our predicament. She had seen these tough times before. Catching up and making a decent living at Fayette would be difficult or impossible. There was not enough land. I began to worry. I loved it there. Leaving would be hard. But my wife hated it. The dilapidated old house, the hazards to the kids' safety, the tumbledown sheds and barns, the nearby river, snakes, abandoned wells and cellars, and timbered ravines. To me, a fixer-upper paradise, it was.

One day my cousin Richard drove up. Richard had closed his Dairy Queen in Dickinson for the season and was out selling Franz oil filters. Richard was always selling stuff. I told him I had no money to buy his oil filter. He looked around at my wreckage of a farmyard and nodded in agreement. "Sell this pile of junk and get a DQ and make some money," he said. "You got these kids you can put to work. You'll make more money in one year than you will here in five."

"I don't even know what a milkshake or a cheeseburger is," I retorted.

"I'll send one of my top girls, Darlene, to teach you," Richard said. "Jamestown and Miles City are for sale. Go take a look at them. I'll go with you," he said. He quoted me the sales and profit numbers of his little DQ operation, and I became very interested. My passion for fixing up Fayette sort of waned. To make a long story short, I decided on a Dairy Queen in Miles City, Mont. Thus began the transition from Fayette to a successful career in the milkshake and cheeseburger selling business. Thank you, Richard. I'll be forever grateful. . . .

That is not the end of the Fayette story, though. What I couldn't have known was that years later, the oil rights I had retained on the land and passed on to my children would become very valuable. Ultimately, Fayette was not a failure at all. Who could have known?

From the Farm to Fast Food

Our new neighbors in Miles City, Mont., the Jerrels and the Sanwalds, must have been alarmed. A couple with eight kids moving into a small house between them next door. There goes the neighborhood. This guy plans on making a living running the little seasonal ice cream stand down the street. Good luck with that.

The neighbors had reason for concern. The forlorn little DQ was a long shot. Innovation was needed. Cousin Richard offered a plan that worked for him. Introduce a tasty, fast, easy-to- prepare item: the DQ BBQ, a seasoned, ground-beef sandwich in a toasted bun for 19 cents. It worked. Soon carloads of school students were making daily lunch trips to our little DQ, as were nearby shopping center employees, construction workers, and area ranchers, who were glad we were selling and promoting their beef. A couple of 19-cent BBQs and a 30-cent milkshake—it was a 68-cent meal fit for a king. The beef and bun suppliers were kind enough to extend credit when times were tough at first. Thank you, Mr. Munsell.

By 1969, we needed a larger building. The banker said "No," when I asked about financing. But the previous owner of the DQ, Mr. Harbec, heard of this plan and loaned me the money. Thank you, Mr. Harbec. We closed the little ice cream stand in October and started building. By mid-March, we had a neat new red barn with an attached dining room seating 64. It was the newest, neatest Dairy Queen in Montana. A dream come true.

We needed to thank all of our loyal customers and entice new ones. A sundae giveaway should do it. I ordered 12 cases of cups and spoons and lots of toppings, and we had a two-day "Come and Get 'em" free sundae shindig. No limit. Come one, come all, the flavor of your choice. We gave away 10,000 sundaes. The town was littered with cups with the Dairy Queen logo on each one. We were on our way. Whoopie!

But it would not have been possible without the hard work of Marie, my crew, and my kids, Raymond, Cindy, Mary, Rita, Lucy, Tommy, Julie, and Amy. We dressed Amy, age 6, up in a white outfit like the rest of the crew, and she was interviewed by the local TV station, which was doing a live telecast of our DQ sundae extravaganza.

The new Dairy Queen. It was a very popular place. Not a gold mine, but definitely a profitable "gut mine."

CATTLE RUSTLING AT THE DAIRY QUEEN

Not much vandalism occurred during our years in Miles City. One obscenity on the ladies restroom was all, and some guy scribbled "Buy a mirror, you cheapskate," on the men's restroom wall where I had forgotten to put one. (I took care of it.) And the fiberglass calf got stolen. I bought a life-sized fiberglass cow and calf to create a dairy farm scene in the grassy area in front of the DQ. There also was a windmill. All this was within a rail fence. Children enjoyed crawling around on the cows, riding them, and posing for pictures their parents were clicking. These plastic animals were not animated and did not move as they were bolted to concrete anchors.

One morning the calf was gone. Stolen! What would anyone do with it? Display it in their front yard? Hardly. I hoped it would be returned, but it wasn't. One day a customer called me aside and said, "Ray, you will find your calf in the ravine north of 4th Street." I thanked him and fetched the calf. It was not damaged, so we replanted it next to the mama cow.

Hobos and Other Different DQ Customers

In my years in business I have seen a variety of interesting folks. Let me tell you about a few more of them. Twice a year royalty(?) graced the dining room of our Dairy Queen in Miles City, He was the nationally acclaimed and duly elected king of the hobos, the Pennsylvania Kid. A colorful character he was. Feathers, flowers, beads, and buttons adorned his ragged attire. He was a sight to behold.

The Pennsylvania Kid would sit around for hours in the dining room, posing for photos with curious tourists. Children sat on his lap, and he told them stories of his hobo life. People would give him money, of course. Our restaurant may have been one of his most profitable locations. He seemed happy with his chosen "profession" and his reign as king. On his last trek, he said he was thinking of retiring if he could find a rich woman who would marry him.

Another group of customers were train crews. They would stop the trains, leaving the engines idling, walk over to the DQ, and casually have lunch before proceeding to Chicago or wherever.

One hot summer day, an old shabby panel-style delivery truck stopped at the DQ. Several spare tires were strapped to the front. A crude rack on the top was stacked with chests, furniture, and a variety of old stuff. The license plate on the truck read "Tennessee." A weary looking couple scanned the menu, which was posted on a billboard on the side of the DQ. A bunch of little faces peered from behind them. They consulted their budget. She came in and ordered twenty-five 19-cent BBQs to go. He filled jugs from the water fountain, and they drove away, heading west.

A similar incident: An old Ford Falcon, a tiny little economy car, pulling a large farm wagon loaded with a family's belongings heading for Seattle. I cringed at the thought of this rig crossing the Rockies. They must have made it. No news of a wreck. . . .

The Robot Man

Richard was his name. He resembled politician John McCain in stature and was about 40 years old. Richard walked like a robot, as though he had no knees or elbows and always in a straight line: east, west, north, or south. But never diagonally. He always looked very angry. People avoided him, and he never had a job that anyone knew of. He spent his time at the library reading. He lived with his mother, he said.

Richard came to the DQ often, his favorite order being a banana split and large coke. He asked that it be served on a tray. At the table he sat and studied it, turning the tray many directions, peering at it from various angles, as though he was planning the best place to start eating, all the while wiping his hands with numerous napkins. He would rearrange the two items on that tray a dozen times before he picked a place to start. Another dilemma: What to eat first? Strawberries, chocolate, or pineapple? These were serious issues. Life was hard for Richard.

One day my daughter Mary, who worked at the DQ, asked Richard, "How are you today, sir?" He told her in scientific terms she did not understand, using words as long as ax handles. It took him a half an hour after factoring in his age, the weather, his zodiac sign, the average temperature for the area, and the time of year. On another day Richard asked me for a job application. I told him, "Sorry, Richard. You would not fit in here."

"I understand that, Mr. Schmidt," he replied. "But could you write a note stating that I applied, but no job was available? I am required to submit proof that I was seeking employment in order to receive assistance." It was rumored that Richard had tried to enroll in

Montana State University several times but was never accepted. Too bad. A potentially great mind gone to waste.

The Miles City Hillbillies

Soon after moving to Miles City, I came up behind this: A rototiller-type of tractor pulling a two-wheel trailer down the middle of the street. It was driven by a bearded old guy smoking a pipe and a little old lady, a mutt dog between them. Sitting in back facing the rear was a younger guy, also a pipe smoker.

I followed this rig for a ways thinking it would take me to a parade forming, and this would a sort of Beverly Hillbillies float. No luck. They just randomly drove around. Returning to the DQ, I told my employees of this contraption. "Oh, those were the [we won't reveal their names here]," the employee explained. "They drive this rig around all the time. It's their car . . . really! Everyone just goes around them. The police do their best to protect them. They are just a part of the community. They are poor and uneducated, live in a junky old house down by the river, and people give them food and clothing and stuff. Donnie, the guy sitting in the back, is their grandson who lives with them because his retarded mother threw him out into a snow bank when he was a baby because he wouldn't stop crying. The grandparents happened to come by and rescued him. So he lives with them."

Later Donnie would have his own vehicle, which was patterned after Grandpa's. He would come to the DQ and ask if he could "charge it," as he had no money. We said, "Sure," but no one ever kept track. Every month the grandparents would stop by to pay Donnie's bill. They insisted, so a fake number was given them, like 30 cents. Donnie died when he drove his rig too close to the edge and rolled down an embankment. All of Miles City mourned his passing. A lady wrote a poignant eulogy praising Miles City's citizens for their kindness and consideration shown Donnie and his grandparents.

Hobos at a New DQ

The following stories takes place in Laurel, Mont., a railroad town and hobo haven. Marie and I owned and operated a Dairy Queen and lived there for five years after selling the DQ in Miles City. There is a large railyard across from Main Street in downtown Laurel. It's a noisy, busy area day and night. Boxcars banging into each other as they are hitched together to form up trains. Some are a mile long. Maybe more. Switch engines rumble back and forth, blowing their horns, and clanging bells. Sometimes extra locomotives, two or three of them, known as "slaves" are added to provide the extra power needed to pull their cargos westward over the Rocky mountain passes. Trains roll in and out in all directions. North, south, east, and west. Railroading is the lifeline for Laurel. No one is likely to complain about the racket and smoke generated by trains.

All the trains stop at Laurel to change crews, reroute box cars, and refuel locomotives, etc. This interval creates a harbor for hobos. They like towns where trains stop and go. "Traveling by rail beats the hell out of hitchhiking on the highway," a hobo told me. "Much more reliable. You can rest a little and get a bite to eat.

So, almost every day during the summer months hobos, aka bums, visit lovely Laurel. Lots of them. They wander through the alleys behind Main Street. Meanwhile, cafes and restaurants and the Dairy Queen on Main cater to hungry train crews.

The trash dumpsters in the alleys behind these dining places also provide an abundant smorgasbord of discarded food remnants for this parade of forlorn, aimless human beings, who, due to circumstances of their own making or beyond their control, are unable to blend in with society, fall through the cracks, and survive on the leftovers of others, who are generous and willing to provide a handout. Some are too proud to beg, shunning the humiliation of the act. Others are fearful of being arrested and jailed for vagrancy. Many appear to be mentally handicapped.

The beggars who came to the Laurel DQ were given a cheeseburger and a milkshake. A royal treat for a king of the road? Often we asked these uninvited drop-in guests to please dine outside at the picnic table instead of in the dining room, the issue being personal hygiene. The diesel exhaust fumes belching out of locomotives is not kind or concerned about the health maintenance of unticketed passengers riding in or on top of boxcars rolling thousands of miles over the Rocky Mountains in the west, then across the vast plains, the prairies and badlands of the Dakotas on the way to the big cities in the east. A beggar disembarking from a freight train is not likely to be welcome at restaurants where bathed, lotioned, perfumed folks dined, especially on hot summer days. I became fascinated with this hobo culture. The following are stories about a few who visited us at the Laurel DQ.

The Napkin Novelist

"Mr.Schmidt," complained Brian, a DQ employee, "There's this hobo sitting in the corner booth. He's been there since we opened. We gave him something to eat, and now he's sitting there writing stuff on napkins, using up a bunch of them. It's lunch time and we'll need that booth. And it's a mess, and the place is filling up with people. How do we get him out of there?"

"I'll take care of it, Brian," I said. I confronted this hobo author, a handsome, happy-looking chap, but totally filthy. He looked to be about 30 years old. He was kind of young compared to his fellow nomads on the road. He was busily scribbling on napkins, having raided the dispensers from nearby tables. Piles of napkins were stacked around him, as well as scattered over the floor. He looked up at me and said, "Hello there! Nice place you got here." He grinned and said, "You must be the boss, right?"

"Yes I am. It looks like you're writing a novel on our napkins," I commented.

His eyes brightened, "How did you guess? That's exactly what I'm writing. Yes, a novel. A real novel," he exclaimed.

"Is that so?" I inquired. What will your novel written on my napkins be about?"

"It's about the biblical prostitute Mary Magdalen. You know they stoned her to death." He looked sad momentarily and then continued. "And I don't think that was right, and I am going to vindicate her. She got a bum rap, that's what she got. And someone needs to do something and that will be me."

"Sounds OK to me," I said. "But I need this booth, so you'll have to write the rest of the novel somewhere else."

"Oh certainly," he said. Then he gathered up all the chapters of his manuscript, stuffing them into a bag and started for the door. Before exiting he turned, grinned at me, and waved. "Good day, sir, and thank you." And then he was gone.

How can anyone not love a bum who's on a mission to exonerate Mary Magdalen on Dairy Queen napkins?

The Dumpster Diner

One cold and windy day, I looked out the window and observed a hobo reaching into the trash dumpster in the alley behind the DQ. These trash bins are about four-feet tall and three-foot in diameter. The hobo was kind of a short guy. It was a long reach. He lost his balance and tumbled into it. He didn't reappear for quite some time, so I decided I better check. When I got there he was sitting amid the trash munching on the remnants of a hot dog. I offered to help him out of his predicament, but he shook his head. He told me he hadn't slept well last night and was tired and going to take nap in there. "I'm outta the wind, and the warm sun is shining in. It's nice, real nice," he said.

I reminded him this may not be a good option because the city garbage truck would be along soon, and the driver may not see him and dump him with the garbage, which might be a messy and possibly fatal for him. He nodded. I helped him out, and Helen, our employee, brought him a burger and shake. He thanked us and went on his way to who knows where? "On the road again?" Maybe I saved his life. We'll never know. Suffocating inside a garbage truck would be a horrible way to die. Even a hobo deserves better than that.

Lady Hobos

Lady hobos. What would they be called? Hobettes? Shebos? Take your pick. Here are the stories of two women whose travels took them through Laurel, Montana. They dropped in for lunch and more at the Dairy Queen.

One of the women came in late on a rainy night. She was quite

FROM THE FARM TO FAST FOOD

tall and slender, about 30 years of age, although it was hard to tell. She was cold, wet, and dirty. She wore ill-fitting shabby clothing and a baseball cap, and was carrying a plastic trash bag. She sat down in a booth by a window and stared out into the cold, dark, drizzly night. Her beautiful but dirty face reflected weariness, despair, and desperation. Marie came with hot soup, coffee, and a sandwich. She nodded in gratitude. She ate slowly and kept looking out the window, oblivious of the time. We had closed at 10 P.M. The doors were locked. All the customers had gone. The cleanup was done, and we wanted to go home. Our guest seemed in no hurry to leave when she finished eating. She just sat and looked out the window.

Marie said, "Go talk to her, Ray." So I did.

"I'm sorry Ma'am, but you'll have to leave now. We're closed and want to go home," I announced in my most authoritative tone of voice. Kicking people out of the DQ was something I didn't like doing. And now this. A woman hobo.

She nodded, got up, took her bag and started for the door. A light rain was falling and the temperature was near freezing.

"Where will you go? Do you have a place to spend the night?" I inquired. She shrugged and shook her head. This woman had not uttered a single word since she walked in the door. It made me wonder if she was mute. I gave her $10 and directed her to an old hotel a block away. This was the price of a room there. I watched to make sure that she got there.

The next morning, shortly after we opened the DQ for business, this lady traveler came back and sat down. Why waste a good thing? She was cleaned up and looked ready to face the challenges of the day. After partaking of another Dairy Queen meal, she thanked us and resumed her journey, a nomad walking down the highway to wherever it led. It was a nice day. She walked westward. The sun shining on the mountain-tops in the distance created a lovely view for her.

TAKING A BATH AT THE DAIRY QUEEN

This is a short story. It won't take long to read. It's kind of funny, although our employee Judy would not agree. She shrieked and came bounding from the ladies restroom, where she had gone to clean up after the DQ closed one night.

"There's a big black naked lady in there!" Judy blurted out hysterically. "I opened the door and there she was, and she yelled at me, 'Git outta here! Can't you see I'm taking a bath?'"

"What are you saying, child?" asked Marie. (She calls everybody child; it must be the mother thing in her) "There's someone in the ladies room naked"?

"Yes," wailed Judy. "She's taking a sponge bath. Scared me half to death! What are we going to do?"

"Oh my gosh. I don't know. Well, let's just wait a while," Marie advised.

We busied ourselves with other tasks and kept an eye on that restroom door. The good-sized lady emerged shortly thereafter. She walked nonchalantly out the door without even asking for something to eat. Cleanliness trumped hunger. Goodbye, lady hobette. Have a safe trip.

A Hobo from Heaven?

This one made me nervous. He walked into the DQ one cold evening and took a seat at the far corner of the room. This man had the face of Jesus. He looked just like the depiction of Jesus Christ. Long flowing hair, a beard, and Arabic facial features. And those intent piercing eyes, which he kept focused on me. Staring at me constantly.

He coughed a lot and seemed to be ill. Our employee Helen brought coffee and food to him, which he slowly ate, watching me all the time. When he finished he remained seated until closing time, sipping coffee and coughing and staring at me.

"This guy gives me the creeps," I complained to Marie in the back room. "I feel like God sent him here with a message or something. Are we are going to kick him out into the cold, he's obviously sick."

Marie went to our apartment for a heavy army blanket and gave it to him. He nodded and walked out. A week later he was back, less the blanket. He munched another free meal and was gone. We never saw him again. This Jesus lookalike haunts me to this day. Was there a message here? We did have a spare bedroom in our apartment.

The Dollar-Hating Hobo

One day I encountered another hobo in the alley going through the DQ's trash bin. He looked to be about 40, although it's hard to read those weather-beaten faces. I had three one-dollar bills in my pocket, which I handed him. He slapped my hand, sending the bills fluttering to the street. Then he proceeded to stomp them with the heel of his tattered shoe, all the while ranting and cussing them dollars.

"Don't be giving me any filthy money, mister," he stormed. "Damn filthy stuff is the root of all evil. It's the reason for all the misery and the killing and murdering." He spit down at them innocent one dollar bills, kicked them aside, and walked down the alley toward the next dumpster.

A Young Hitchhiker

This one was did not fit the profile of the hobo culture. He looked kind of young and innocent. He was hitchhiking the Interstate highway instead of the rails. For his own safety I thought this was good planning.

I was traveling between Billings and Miles City, Montana. I picked him up as he was walking westward. He climbed into the pickup beside me, plopped his gunny sack onto the floorboards leaned back, and fell asleep. I glanced at him. A teenaged kid. Running away from home perhaps.

As we neared Billings, I woke him up. I wanted to visit with my young passenger. Here's his story: He said he was 16 years old and from Dayton, Ohio. His single mother, with whom he was living, had died. He knew nothing at all about his father. He thought, but wasn't sure, he had a sister in Seattle and was going there to look for her. I reminded him that Seattle was a big city and this might be impossible, but he was undaunted. "She's out there somewhere, and I'll find her," he asserted. I dropped him off at the Laurel exit. I often wonder if I did the right thing.

Thank God for Hobos

It was Thanksgiving Day and the DQ was closed. These are days to repair and fix things, which I was doing. The employees were enjoying a day off. I was fixing stuff. That's the way it usually works.

I glanced out the window and observed a hobo digging through the dumpster in the alley.

"A hell of way for a man to get Thanksgiving dinner," I muttered. "Poor guy."

Later in the morning Marie came by from our apartment and invited me to go to dinner at the nearby Owl Cafe. I gladly accepted her invitation. As we were eating dinner in this crowded cafe, a cowboy entered. With him was the hobo I had seen earlier in the alley. "Sit down in a booth and I will buy you dinner," the cowboy said to the hobo. "And behave yourself and don't give anybody any s—t," (is the word he used). Tough talk.

The Owl had a counter with stools in addition to booths and tables. There were a number of railroad men sitting at this counter. Among them was an elderly man who began to choke on his food. He was gasping and struggling for breath. Everyone in the place was transfixed, frozen in their seats, except the hobo. The hobo instantly bounded to the man's side and whacked him on the back, dislodging the offending food. Then he proceeded to clean the old gentleman up with napkins, comforted and calmed him, and asked him if he was OK.

He went back to his booth and finished his dinner. When he was done, he thanked the cowboy and the waitress, bummed a cigarette and light from a smoker seated near the door, and walked out the door and crossed the street toward the trains. Just a walking along, whistling a song. An unsung, unknown, hobo hero on a Thanksgiving Day, he was.

Questions to Enhance Your Book Club

1. Which parts of the book made you laugh?
2. Which parts of the book made you sad? Why?
3. Was there anything about this book that changed how you think about life? If so, what?
4. What stories in the book did you find to be the most educational or surprised you about how people lived in decades past?
5. What do you think children and young people could learn from this book?
6. The author argues that big families are an asset. Is he right or wrong? What are the pros and cons of big families today versus past generations?

A Conversation with the Author

What inspired you to write this book?
I wanted to put my memories on paper for others to read and be entertained and informed about how life was in the era in which I grew up. Like a lot of people, Steinbeck's *The Grapes of Wrath* inspired me, but I wanted to tell my stories with a bit of humor.

Do you consider yourself a good storyteller
No. I stammer and use the wrong words. Writing is better for me. I can erase and redo what I have written until I like it. It took many hours to put my thoughts into a correct form. I still have a problem doing this.

What did you like best about writing the book?
The feeling that I was realizing a life-long dream—writing a book. I decided to do that when I was a kid.

What did you like the least?
My two-finger typing was, and is, agonizingly slow and frustrating. Learning to work my new computer has made it even tougher.

Was it hard to write about your own life? Which parts did you find it difficult to write about?
No. I found it very fulfilling to be able to do it. But writing about my brother Philip's birth and death was kind of hard. Writing about my losing my fingers and what happened to me when I worked at the post office was very difficult. My kids pestered me to include these stories in the book for better or worse. I did. I hope they made the right call.

What would you like readers to get out of this book?
I hope older readers enjoy reliving the era I wrote about. I think younger readers—even those who are knowledgeable about it—will be in for many surprises about how people actually lived back in the "good old days."

Made in the USA
Lexington, KY
15 April 2013